© PD Publishing LTD
Bert Youell has asserted his right to be identified
as the author of this work. Edited by Ian Sealey.

First published in April 2022

British Library Cataloguing in Publication Data
A catalogue record for this book is available
from the British Library.

ISBN 978-1-8384112-5-1

Published by PD Publishing,
Shenvallah, The Green, Dauntsey, Wiltshire, SN15 4HY
Tel: 01666 510 513
Int. tel: +44 1666 510 513
Website: www.prodetailermagazine.com

Printed and bound in the United Kingdom

While every effort is taken to ensure the accuracy of the
information given in this book, no liability can be accepted
by the author or publishers for any loss, damage or injury
caused by errors in, or omissions from the information given.
No animals were harmed during the making of this book,
however a Corgi did get a little bit fat.

HAND WASH ONLY

CONTENTS

WHAT IS DETAILING?

The term 'car detailing' has gradually worked its way into the automotive vernacular since the mid 2000s, and while it has become familiar to any petrolhead, there are many different definitions; even if you ask industry veterans, their answers vary.

In the USA 'car detailing' refers to anything related to washing vehicles, be it an automatic tunnel wash or the artisanal preparation of the world's finest motorcars for concours competitions. In the UK, it is seen as car washing in its most prestigious and pedantic form; a level above car valeting and a long way from the car park wash 'n' go.

Some of the world's top detailers have even started to distance themselves from the term 'detailer' in favour of 'car care professional' or 'vehicle appearance specialist' to avoid confusion and association with mere 'car washers'. In the USA, if you ask for a valet for your car, someone will take your keys and drive your car away, and you'll need to tip them to get it back.

So, when are you washing a car, when are you valeting one, and when are you 'detailing'? The answer is more existential – it's not *what* you are doing, it's *how* you're doing it.

If you regard the car-washing process as a chore, which involves absent-mindedly wiping an old sponge over your car to either make it look half-respectable or to avoid other household tasks, then you're not 'doing detailing' – in fact you may well be making work for a detailer by damaging the paint. However, if you have set aside a whole weekend in the calendar to prepare your pride and joy, if you have looked forward to some 'us time' with your four-wheeled friend, and if you have more products and equipment for vehicular cleanliness than you do for your own personal hygiene and grooming, the chances are that you've got the existential attitude of a detailer, and this book will be for you!

Ultimately, we want to take a car in its current condition and transform its physical appearance into a better-than-new state. To achieve this, we need to split the procedure into stages, divide these stages into a series of processes, and then show you how and why they should be completed.

We have divided the exterior detailing into four conventional stages: wash, decontamination, correction and protection. We have also included two further sections that cover the interior, engine bay, trim, glass, and other ancillary surfaces that benefit from beautification. We start with an equipment list for each section, and we have presented each process in a series of steps, the latter of which don't always have to be completed should you not have the time, patience or confidence quite yet.

Before we get into that, we need to touch on health and safety… boring as it may be, the fact remains that we are using all sorts of chemicals, some of which are

⬆ Detailing has become a passion for both amateurs and professionals.

really quite nasty, and we are doing so in the home environment where there are pets, children and potentially even the in-laws. Keep all of your car care products in a high cupboard, even if you are a short person, as they might work well *on* your Rover Vitesse but they aren't so great *in* Rover, the Labrador. Furthermore, do take care of the second most important thing in your life after the aforementioned motorcar: you! Reputable products will have safety guidance printed on their labels, and it should be followed. We have seen all manner of burns and rashes as a consequence of people not wearing gloves, let alone eye damage from not wearing safety goggles, and worst of all, respiratory damage from not wearing masks. While we hope to provide you with plenty of first date conversation topics in this book, your consequentially increased allure may well be counteracted if your visage has been singed with tar remover.

Chapter 1

EQUIPMENT ESSENTIALS

The first step is to ensure you have the chemicals and equipment needed. There are quite literally thousands of chemicals and products available to the detailing enthusiast, and while we have made product suggestions here and there, they are by no means final or exhaustive.

With the right skills you can detail a car with (almost) any products; without the skills you are unlikely to achieve satisfactory results, even with the best products.

Build your equipment portfolio as you develop your skillset – do not feel obliged to go out and splurge on thousands of pounds worth of equipment before mastering the two-bucket method.

WASH KIT LIST

At a very basic level you will need two buckets, both at least 20 litres in capacity, equipped with grids in the base to trap dirt. Even an entry-level pressure washer will make your life easier, and a snow foam lance should be high on your buy list. A noodle wash mitt has been shown to be the safest contact wash medium you can use, and helpfully they can be found for less than five pounds, though wool and microfibre alternatives are preferred by some. A set of brushes can be useful for the wash process, ideally circular and soft – there are plenty on the market specifically for car care. You might want some chemical-resistent brushes too, though these are rarely soft enough for all tasks.

Conventionally a chamois leather has been favoured to dry vehicles, however, it is so much safer to use a plush microfibre towel, as it is less likely to hold residual grit against the paint and cause damage. For your wheels, there are a plethora of brushes available but wool or microfibre options with long handles make for kinder cleaning.

Chemical-wise, an automotive shampoo is a must – don't be tempted to grab your dish soap! If you have procured a foam lance it would be sensible to purchase some snow foam to go with it, though shampoo will work through the lance too, and many prefer to use a citrus pre-wash via pump sprayer in lieu.

➡ Scratch Shield (left) and Grit Guard (right) both make bucket grids.

⬇ Using two buckets makes the wash process safer, and use a third for wheels.

⬆ The guard sits at the bottom of the wash bucket

➡ The sponge is no longer the stalwart of car washing, usurped by microfibre, wool, and chenille.

A dedicated wheel cleaner isn't essential but is a worthy investment, while a quick detailer (QD) or rinse aid can speed up the drying process.

For those wanting to protect the environment, it is worth considering a containment mat to place under the car to catch all the chemicals and muck so it can be disposed of via the sewerage system down a foul drain rather than leach into the soil and storm drains. If operating commercially, this becomes compulsory.

➡ Soft bristled detailing brushes are perfect for agitating dirt from panel gaps and window rubbers.

⬇ Wheel brushes enable you to clean the inner barrel of many alloy types.

⬆ A pump sprayer is very useful for the pre-wash.

⬅ A foam lance is an effective way of applying a variety of products.

⬇ A containment mat can help to reduce your environmental impact.

DECONTAMINATION KIT LIST

Think of the decontamination process as a 'deep clean'. Decontamination is traditionally split into three stages, each of which require specific chemicals. For tar removal it will come as no surprise that you will need a tar remover product, and the same goes for fallout removal, though these are often referred to as 'iron removers'. To remove bonded contamination, such as some types of tree sap or old wax, you are best off using clay media, be this a clay bar, mitt, pad or cloth. Whichever you choose will require a good clay lubricant, though in extremes you can use a diluted shampoo. Equipment wise: brushes and microfibre cloths are the stalwart and nitrile gloves are a must, as we are starting to use rather more aggressive chemicals than simple detergents.

⬆ Clay pads are easy to use, and potentially safer than old-school clay bars as they can be cleaned.

➡ Warm water can help soften a clay bar prior to use.

⬇ Outside of detailing, few know about the existence of fallout remover products.

CORRECTION KIT LIST

There is no 'complete' list for what you need to machine polish a car as there are so many products out there. Some detailers will insist that you *have* to have everything before so much as musing about machine polishing, whereas many get results using little more than a polishing machine, a foam pad, and some polish. In reality, you don't need to purchase a £2,000 ultrasonic paint depth gauge if you plan to take a small Dual Action polishing machine to your own car with some finishing polish; but if you want to wet sand a supercar it would be foolish not to invest in such equipment.

➡ Paint depth gauges vary in price from under £100 (left) to over £2,000 (right).

⬇ Your paint correction equipment should grow organically with your experience.

In simple terms you will need a machine polisher, a selection of polishing pads that offer different levels of cut, a selection of compounds (polish), some panel wipe and plenty of fresh microfibres. If you are starting out, focus on softer pads and finishing compounds – you don't need to use heavy-cut pads and

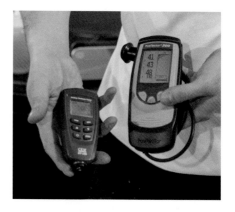

polish, but you will always need to use finer-cut options.

Perhaps more importantly, you will need a suitable environment – ideally under cover and free of dust and damp, with good lighting and plenty of space around the car. While a professional detailing studio will have a wide array of different light sources, having a single mobile LED light is pretty much essential, even for the home enthusiast. We cover the topic in depth later.

On a personal safety note, polishing creates dust and polishes contain solvents. You would be a fool not to spend a couple of pounds on FFP3 (or higher-rated) paper masks and some safety glasses from your local hardware store. Those with pre-existing conditions like asthma would be well advised to take further precautions, such as a more substantial respirator rated to A2P2 or above. Gloves are another essential item; nitrile versions are best suited for detailing.

⬅ There is a huge variety of polishing machines on the market.

⬆ There is also a vast range of different pads on the market.

⬇ Remember to protect yourself, as well as the vehicle, when detailing.

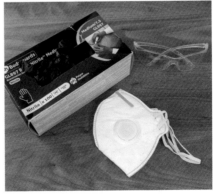

PROTECTION KIT LIST

When it comes to paint protection you have many options ranging from a traditional organic wax through to cutting-edge ceramic coatings. Waxes and polymer sealants are generally easy to apply, tolerant of environmental conditions, and can last from a matter of weeks to over a year. More advanced polymer and 'ceramic' coatings require more preparation, specific environmental conditions and often considerably more patience. In return, they can offer a greater level of protection for a longer period. We will go through the topic in much more depth, but in terms of equipment, clean, soft microfibres and applicator foams are pretty much all you need this side of top-end ceramics.

➡ There is a variety of paint protection product types on the market, from waxes to ceramic coatings.

ENGINE BAY KIT LIST

The single most useful bit of hardware for a typical engine bay is a steamer, which can both speed up the process and can negate the need for more aggressive cleaning chemicals. A wide selection of brushes will also make life easier, and a simple tool kit to undo engine covers and ancillaries can facilitate better access.

When working under the bonnet most of the heavy lifting is done by all-purpose cleaners, while the more stubborn oil and grease demands a degreaser. Brake cleaner can be a useful aid, when used with care, and given the amount of plastic cladding common to a typical modern car, a plastic dressing is handy. For older vehicles with more metal on display, a metal polish and sealant will help, and for those with lots of exposed paint and chrome, a high temperature paste wax can add that final extra 5%.

INTERIOR KIT LIST

A vacuum cleaner really is essential for interior work, while plenty of brushes and microfibres will also aid the process. Consider vacuums with long hoses, a decent crevice tool and other brush accessories. A steamer can be a great investment, and a wet vac is particularly useful on heavily soiled interiors and those with fabric seats.

Chemical-wise, essentially all you need is an all-purpose cleaner (APC) that you can dilute to different concentrations for different applications. However, if you have leather seats, a proper leather cleaner is pretty essential, and there are lots of anti-static trim dressings that keep dust away for longer and leave pleasant aromas. If you have Alcantara in your car, there are a range of specialist products available for when water isn't quite enough.

⬆ The pre-wash is all about removing loose contamination.

Chapter 2

THE WASH PROCESS

The distinction between washing and detailing cars starts with the very first steps of cleaning a car. For many, the primary objective of washing a car is to make it look clean, probably as quickly and painlessly as possible, so they can get back into the warm.

For a detailer it is about removing as much dirt as possible, but not at the cost of causing damage to the paint – there is a decontamination process to get a vehicle truly clean. The wash is more a matter of getting acquainted with a vehicle and removing the first layer of grime.

THE PRE-WASH

Before firing up the pressure washer, make sure the car is parked away from direct sunlight and that the paintwork is cool to the touch. Washing a hot car is possible, but inadvisable, as the chemicals will react in a less controllable manner and are liable to dry out before you get the chance to rinse, leading to residue spots.

If you plan to use a water containment mat, now is the time to set it up, and if you don't, do at least check to ensure run-off water and chemicals aren't going to contaminate flower beds or nearby watercourses, or stain tarmac driveways.

The role of the pre-wash is to remove as much loose dirt as possible from the vehicle without actually touching it with our hands, and it relies primarily on chemical processes and water pressure. A pre-wash product is anything that can be sprayed onto the vehicle, left to loosen and break down dirt chemically and be rinsed off.

The most common pre-wash chemical is snow foam – essentially a detergent that is designed to be used with a foam lance and pressure washer, which 'clings' to the paintwork for between three and ten minutes in order to soften mud and other 'loose' contamination.

⬇ Snow foam is always a crowd-pleaser.

There are hundreds of snow foams on the market, but they can be broadly divided into pH neutral, slightly caustic and slightly acidic. The former won't clean as well as the latter, but supposedly will be kinder to any existing wax or protection you may have on the vehicle.

← The sills and bottoms of doors are always susceptible to picking up loose contamination.

Top Tip

Remember the lower sections of the car and the wheel arches usually get the most clotted mud and detritus. Sometimes it is worthwhile to apply citrus pre-wash to these lower sections after snow foaming and rinsing the whole car. A stubby attachment to your pressure washer is useful for getting between the wheel and the wheel arch.

Top Tip

When applying snow foam, start from the bottom of the car and work up so you can ensure full coverage. When rinsing, start at the top and rinse down to ensure the dirt that is being removed from the upper areas is rinsed off the lower areas.

Detailers also use alternative pre-wash products, not just snow foam, some of which are citrus-based. These can be applied straight from the bottle with a trigger spray, or via a pump sprayer, though many are supplied in a concentrated form that should be diluted as per the instructions. Being a liquid, it tends not to cling to the surface as well as foam but it potentially has greater cleaning power. Applying this to window trims, badges, trim strips and other intricate areas and then gently agitating with a brush can be an effective way to remove dirt without causing damage.

↓ Detailing brushes are great for intricate areas.

With both snow foam and citrus pre-wash, be sure to dilute the product as the manufacturer recommends and leave to 'dwell' as per the instructions. When using it through a foam lance, remember that the lance itself will further dilute the product – usually between ten and twenty times depending on the flow-rate of your pressure washer and the concentration setting on your lance. On some devices, turning the adjustment knob towards the minus sign *increases* the concentration, as the minus and plus symbols refer to water flow *not* concentration of the chosen chemical. Check how yours works before using it.

Top Tip

When calculating a suitable dwell time for any product, especially pre-wash products, take the ambient temperature into account. On warmer days the active ingredients will react faster and their water content will evaporate more quickly, thus they don't need as long as on colder days. As the water content of chemicals evaporates off, they become more concentrated, potentially causing damage – this is why you never let a product dry!

Do not dry the car after the pre-wash – there will still be lots of dirt on the vehicle; the drying process will likely abrade the surface causing swirl marks and damage. Now it is time to move on to the main wash stage, but first let's look at pressure washers and wheel cleaning.

Pressure washers explained

Pressure washers have been around since the late 1920s but it was Alfred Kärcher who has been credited with the first modern device back in 1950. The German company he founded in 1935 has gone on to dominate the pressure washer market with their distinctive yellow domestic machines and grey professional alternatives, but there are now dozens of other manufacturers vying for your custom including Nilfisk, Kranzle and Bosch.

When choosing your own pressure washer there are various things to consider. Stick to your budget; it is all too easy to get drawn into ever more impressive bits of machinery with features that you may not actually need or benefit from. Next come the practical considerations – how long is the hose? How heavy is the machine? Will it work with your power source and water pressure? Finally, once you have the list down to a couple of contenders, it is worth picking one with metal internals and a decent warranty – they can and do go wrong, so build quality and manufacturer support is useful.

For washing, you don't want or need too much pressure, and while a hot water pressure washer makes sense for big commercial car-washing bays, the cost is tough to justify for a home user.

← **Professional machines like this Kranzle are designed to last longer than domestic alternatives.**

As you will likely be using a snow foam lance, the option to add chemicals directly into the machine is often redundant for detailers, though perhaps useful if you plan to use it on your driveway too.

↑ Wheels are often just as delicate as the paintwork.

Top Tip

Remember to always empty the machine of water after use, and at all costs, ensure it doesn't freeze – if that means keeping it in the sitting room during winter, so be it!

Wheels

Many presume wheels are coated in much tougher protection than vehicle bodywork and will need more aggressive products and methods to rid them of muck. Being so close to the ground and next to the brake discs means they also get dirty first and tend to attract more obstinate contamination than other parts of a car. However, most wheels are painted or powder-coated metal with clear coat, and need just as much care as the rest of the vehicle.

The first step is to identify what sort of wheels you have – most cars have cast aluminium alloys that have been painted and clear coated. Some have steel rims which either have plastic hub caps or a painted finish. Some of the more exotic cars have diamond-cut aluminium wheels that have a layer of lacquer, and we are even starting to see carbon fibre wheels filter through.

For motorcyclists in particular, there are anodised finishes that are particularly delicate.

While there is no harm in spraying snow foam or citrus pre-wash on your rims during the pre-wash stage, you can make the process more efficient by applying a dedicated wheel cleaner at this stage. (In the rare event you have bare metal or anodised wheels, or carbon ceramic brakes, be very cautious when applying any product that isn't pH neutral – seek advice from the product manufacturer if unsure.) Commercial car washes often use strongly acidic products to quickly clean the wheels, and while there is a legitimate place for acid wheel cleaners, your standard wash is not it. Look for milder alternatives and don't expect a single application to take your wheel from filthy to flawless – they take some effort to get clean.

Once the wheel cleaner has been applied, give it a minute or two for the chemicals to work their magic, before agitating with a detailing brush.

← With this type of brush, make sure the rubber tip protector stays attached to avoid damage.

↑ Be mindful around carbon ceramic brakes when using silicone products.

When doing the face of the wheel, treat them like an analogue clock, and methodically go around clockwise from 6 o'clock to 5 o'clock, making sure you get every spoke. Depending on the wheel design, it helps to have an order to follow for each spoke, e.g. inner edge, left edge, right edge, outer edge, face. It is worth cleaning the face of the wheel first, then rinsing and using a long-handled brush to do the inner barrel, before rinsing again.

If you do the inner barrel first, you risk rubbing the dirty face and causing damage – if the face is clean it is safer. Finally, remember to clean the backs of the spokes – the bits you can't see – either with a microfibre cloth or a right-angled brush. There will be stubborn marks you can't easily remove – do not rub them, rather leave them for the decontamination stage when you can apply specific chemicals to localised areas to assist.

Top Tip

If you find yourself always missing parts of your wheels, consider doing all four, then moving the car forward about a metre (about half the circumference of a typical 18 inch wheel with a 40 section tyre), and then rechecking each wheel for missed areas.

For the lug nut holes, you can use circular brushes or specialist tools such as Dodo Juice Nutt Plugs. If the centre of the wheel has a cover to hide the bolts, it might be wise to remove this so you can clean inside it. Failing to do so might result in dirty water dripping out when you first drive the car and flinging filthy water over the wheels and surrounding bodywork.

Once fully cleaned and rinsed, you will need to dry the wheels to avoid water spots – look for microfibre drying towels that have a high GSM, say anything over 350, and soft edging (or laser-cut 'edgeless' types) – these will be absorbent and safe to use.

← There is a vast array of brushes and tools for cleaning wheels, and having a range of tools for different wheels is a good plan.

THE CONTACT WASH

Ask most people if they know how to wash a car and they will assume you're being patronising, but in fact it is a skill that takes some practice and finesse to do correctly. You are essentially trying to remove dirt without damaging the paint.

Top Tip

Before starting, ensure you are wearing appropriate clothing – if you remain entirely dry after washing a car you are either coated in PTFE or have a very small car. Also remove anything that might scratch the car if you accidentally touch it – belt buckles, watches, rings, etc.

You will need two sturdy buckets for the bodywork and a third for the wheels, ideally of at least 20 litres in volume. The reason detailers use two buckets for the bodywork is to reduce the amount of dirt being re-applied to a car during the wash process. If you have flat-bottomed buckets, as opposed to those with a ridge that lifts the base off the ground, be careful using them on gravel or sharp surfaces as they can split when full.

In 2001, Grit Guard invented a grid that sits in the bottom of the bucket and acts as a baffle plate to keep dirt from your wash media in the bottom of the bucket. Since then, numerous other companies such as Scratch Shield, Detail Guardz and Chemical Guys have brought out alternatives, but whichever you choose, they are a worthwhile purchase for all your buckets.

It is also a good idea to label your buckets to avoid dunking in the wrong one in all the excitement. While 'Mandy' or 'Derek' are options, we would suggest 'Rinse', 'Wash' and 'Wheels' – as companies have already made vinyl stickers for you to use.

Add your shampoo into the 'Wash' bucket, following the manufacturer's advice on quantity, and use your pressure washer to mix and froth the solution. For those in hard water areas you might need to add a little extra – though we all know everyone will add a dollop or two extra as a matter of course.

⬇ Take the time to get the concentration correct when dosing your bucket.

⬆ Wipe in straight, overlapping lines with no pressure.

Dip your chosen wash medium – more about that overleaf – into the wash bucket so it gets fully saturated. Then, starting with the roof, wipe it over the car in a single straight line with just the weight of the wash medium – do not apply any pressure! Overlap the first line with the second to ensure there are no missed areas. Always start at the top of a car and work down, this way you avoid dirt flowing over areas you have just cleaned.

Mentally divide your car into sections that can be wiped without moving or stretching too far – for example, you can divide the roof into two or four sections. Once a section has been wiped, dunk the wash medium into your rinse bucket and give it a scrub with your free hand. Then dunk it in the wash bucket and repeat. Generally, upper parts of the car are cleaner than those closer to the road, so you can do more between 'dunks' than lower down the car. Some people use a different mitt just to do the lower sections – particularly if you are using more expensive and delicate wool mitts for upper areas.

Once complete, rinse the car again just to get rid of the suds and highlight any spots you may have missed. If you have access to filtered water, this would be the time to use it to reduce the chance of water spotting. If you now feel sufficiently invigorated and want to call it a day, you will need to move onto the drying phase. However, if you have found your rhythm and want to continue, the decontamination phase is next. If it is a hot day or you want a breather before carrying on, it still may be worth drying the car to avoid water spots.

⬅ Perhaps use a different wash mitt for lower parts of the car.

↑ Drips of water left on a car, particularly a dark one in warm weather, may look harmless...

↑ Left for just ten minutes, the water evaporates leaving mineral deposits.

Wash media explained

For many years, people used sponges to wash their cars, and indeed, many still do. However, there are safer and more efficient alternatives out there that are well worth considering. The problem with a cheap sponge, and the same goes for a chamois leather, is that they have a habit of holding grit from your car against the paint. When you wipe, you are effectively using the grit as sandpaper and inflicting all sorts of damage to the clear coat of your car.

Wool, synthetic wool and microfibre-based wash pads and mitts are able to hold the grit away from the paint surface, and are safer in this regard, reducing what we call 'wash marring'. Tests have shown that chenille mitts are the safest option in terms of marring, and if you can find decently large versions with the chenille material on the front and back, you won't go far wrong. We prefer mitts to pads as they are harder to drop (though pads hold more soapy water and therefore can provide better lubrication), but if you don't enjoy chenille mitts, it is worth trying other options – there are plenty out there.

➡ Wool wash mitts are popular alternatives to sponges, but they need careful maintenance to ensure longevity.

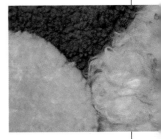

➡ Microfibre wash media are generally easier to maintain than wool.

⬇ Paint marring is often caused by improper wash techniques.

DRYING

More damage to paint seems to occur at the drying phase than during any other wash process, so it is worth taking extra care. Normal microfibres are blended polyester and polyamide fibres arranged in various densities, depending on their intended application. Products marketed as drying towels are typically larger and heavier than more general-purpose alternatives, and often have different textures on each side. Their primary objective is to be as absorbent as possible and they are often the most expensive microfibre a detailer owns.

There are two ways to use a drying towel. The first is the quickest and easiest, where you simply lay the towel on a panel and pull it along by two corners. The second method involves laying the towel onto a panel, leaving it for a couple of seconds and then lifting it off – sometimes patting it gently prior to lifting. The second method is safer as there is no 'dragging' action that could potentially abrade the paint, but it can take much longer. A happy compromise is to spray a very light mist of quick detailer onto the paint before dragging the drying towel over the surface.

⬆ Microfibre drying towels are much safer and more effective to use than chamois leathers.

This acts as a lubricant and makes the first method safer and faster.

There are various other gadgets that can be useful for drying, such as warm air blowers that act in a similar way to a hair dryer. These are very useful for blowing recalcitrant drops of water from door handles, wing mirrors and other crevices. If you're on a budget, pet-drying blowers are effective and affordable; while at the other end of the scale, Bigboi and Air Force Blaster have a range of built-for-purpose blowers that offer greater practicality. Another gadget worth considering is the Dropnetic by Microfiber Madness – think of it as an oversized magnetic pipe cleaner coated in thick microfibre that clings to the side of a steel-bodied car and can be placed under mirrors or door handles to catch any drips. It sounds a little bonkers, but it works.

Top Tip

Be sure to use a simple QD and not a spray sealant, which may contain waxes or sealants that require buffing. Alternatively there are numerous drying aids on the market.

⬅ Air blowers are perhaps the safest drying system.

Chapter 3

THE DECON PROCESS

The decontamination stage is all about removing the bonded dirt that won't come off with a safe wash. As with the wash, the priority is always to remove contamination as safely as possible, starting with the mildest option and then building up to more aggressive alternatives, only if required.

Most of the contamination would be removed by machine polishing, but we always decontaminate prior to machining so the contamination doesn't interfere with the polishing process: a chunk of tar getting stuck to your polishing pad could really spoil your day.

🔺 Decontamination is a methodical process.

The key to decontaminating a car efficiently is to understand the nature of the contaminant and what type of product or process is most effective to remove it. For example, trying to remove road tar with a 'soapy' detergent will likely be long-winded, damaging and ultimately ineffective; however, if you use a solvent designed to break down hydrocarbons, the process becomes a cinch. You also need to consider the secondary effects of products, continuing the tar removal example; some tar-removing solvents can stain plastic and rubber, often turning it white. In this case, the key is to avoid overspray and ensure any excess product is removed and not allowed to drip onto other surfaces.

There are various schools of thought regarding which type of decontamination to remove first, but we normally suggest starting by attacking the largest molecules as they may hide other contamination underneath them, such as fallout particles hiding underneath large tar blobs. Before starting, you really need to consider your personal safety and put on some nitrile gloves and safety glasses at the very least. Childbirth may be painful, but it pales in comparison to the blinding pain of thioglycolic acid on the eyeball.

Broadly speaking, we divide contamination into three categories, listed in descending size order: hydrocarbon (tar, rubber, oil-based substances), organic (tree sap, pollen, insects) and fallout (iron particles and industrial pollution).

HYDROCARBON REMOVAL

Anyone who has owned a light-coloured car will know about the little black spots that stand proud of the paint, often around the wheel arches and lower sections of a car. This is most profound in summer when people wash their cars more often and the bitumen on our roads softens and is more easily 'flicked' onto the bodywork by the tyres. Despite the ready availability of perfectly good tar-removing products, many a home enthusiast has whipped out a Brillo Pad and rubbed them off, along with plenty of surrounding clear coat, leaving a horrible cross-hatched patch of scratches.

On a modern car with 'healthy' paint, you can simply spray a tar remover onto the afflicted areas, leave for a couple of minutes, and then safely wipe off with a microfibre. If the tar doesn't all come off, do not scrub, simply reapply more product and repeat the process. On heavily contaminated cars you may find yourself doing whole panels, with little black spots 'bleeding' brown as they dissolve away. There is nothing wrong with this, though product costs do tend to rise rapidly. However, don't spray a whole car top to bottom and walk off for tea and cake – never let tar remover dry on paintwork and try to avoid getting it on rubber and unpainted trim, particularly chrome-effect or anodised finishes.

A rule of thumb is that the more effective the tar remover (i.e. the faster it dissolves tar and the fewer hits required to remove it), the higher the chances are that it can damage trim, or even delicate clear coat. Look for tar removers that are a little thicker, almost a gel, as they will cling to vertical surfaces for longer and dribble less. If using a more watery product, consider saturating part of a microfibre cloth and gently holding it against the contaminated area for two minutes to work its chemical magic.

Top Tip

When wiping away tar, use little to no pressure and turn your microfibre regularly to prevent chunks of tar abrading the surface. While the tar itself can be damaging, it often holds grit and rock fragments from the road, which aren't softened by the tar remover. Once used for tar removal, a microfibre cloth should only be used for 'dirty' tasks.

⬇ Tar spots bleed brown as they are dissolved.

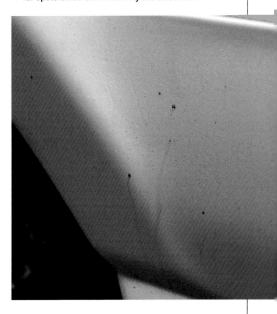

BONDED CONTAMINANT REMOVAL

Bonded contamination is a general term to cover a multitude of stubborn substances that like to adhere themselves to paint. Sap from trees, often excreted by aphids, is perhaps the most common, while the category would also cover things like concrete and paint overspray.

Top Tip

You can tell how badly contaminated your paint is by using a plastic bag – simply insert your finger into the bag and then touch the paintwork with it. The plastic exaggerates the sensation of the contamination, and you can sometimes even hear the difference. Make sure your neighbours aren't watching though, as it's a tough one to explain.

⬇ Place your hand in a thin plastic bag.

⬇ Feel the paintwork with your fingertips through the bag.

The idea of using clay on a car may seem somewhat bizarre but it has been the go-to for detailers since the 1990s. Its origins are quite literally a block of clay, that one warmed and moulded by hand and lightly swiped over the bodywork. While this system is still used, various manufacturers have come up with easier, faster and safer alternatives that still use clay, but in the form of mitts, cloths and even pads for use by machine. The application principle remains the same, gently swiping the clay over the paintwork in straight lines, using no pressure and plenty of lubricant. Clay lubricant is cheap and accessible, so should be used liberally to help minimise the risk of marring. A 1:50 mix of automotive shampoo and water can be used in lieu, but while this can be cheaper, shampoo offers less lubrication so is simply not as good as dedicated clay lube.

As the surface of a clay bar becomes contaminated, fold it into itself and re-flatten it so the contamination is trapped within the clay and there is a clean surface with which to continue.

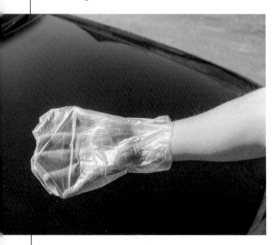

1 Warm the clay in water or with your hands.

2 Spread the clay into a thin palm sized piece.

3 Hold the clay flat in the palm of your hand.

4 Apply clay lube to the clay and the surface to be clayed.

5 Move the clay briskly over the paint in straight lines.

6 You can use a clay cloth as an alternative.

7 Same applies as with a clay bar – straight, overlapping lines.

To clay or not to clay?

However careful you are, it is almost impossible not to generate some clay bar marring, which ranges from a slightly misty, mottled effect (usually the consequence of not warming the clay or being parsimonious with the lube) right through to significant swirls and scratches that glisten in the sunshine, giving a hologram effect. So, if you have a perfectly detailed car and you don't intend to do any machine polishing – perhaps you just want to apply a layer of wax – then it would be advisable not to clay the vehicle.

⬇ Clay bars will need replacing when there is no more uncontaminated surface remaining.

However, if you are going to machine polish the car, clay bar marring will be easy to remove with just a light finishing polish, so it is well worth doing.

Once you have had some practice with the clay bar and aren't removing heavy contamination, you could always hand polish the car to remove almost all evidence of the clay bar. Equally, if the car is already covered in swirls and marks, and the intention is just to make it shiny or hide the marks with a glaze, then a clay bar isn't going to worsen the situation and may help the glaze last a little longer.

FALLOUT REMOVAL

Of all the forms of contamination, fallout particles are usually the smallest and the last that should be attended to, though some like to attack them earlier, even in the pre-wash.

⬇ Fallout particles usually bleed red or purple as they are dissolved.

Fallout refers to miniscule particles of Fe_2 that exist in our atmosphere and settle on everything, including cars. It is usually particularly intense in areas of heavy industry and rail yards as metal-on-metal action releases it into the environment and heavier particles will fall closer to their source.

Fallout particles are also produced by the action of braking, when the brake pads and discs are squeezed together, producing considerable heat and pressure. You will find that high-performance brakes produce more fallout in general, and that carbon ceramic and drum brakes produce much less – that's a first date factoid!

↟ Fallout remover can be used on wheels and bodywork.

Top Tip

If your car is equipped with carbon ceramic brakes, you may hear that the brake discs are particularly vulnerable to acids and other strong chemicals. Acids aren't actually an issue for these, but silicones are, so keep those tyre dressings away! The forged carbon fibre discs and ceramic pads tend to use copper rather than iron in their construction, so they don't produce as much, if any, iron fallout.

Sometimes you can see fallout on paint if you look very closely, but for the most part it is invisible until you start to remove it. To remove fallout, use fallout remover (see, this detailing lark isn't all that difficult) – a solution that contains thioglycolic acid. This acid reduces Fe_2 to Fe_3, which is water-soluble and can be rinsed off. Unlike tar remover, fallout remover is almost always entirely safe to use on plastic, rubber and unpainted parts of the car, so you can spray the whole car safely.

There are two attributes of fallout remover that must be experienced to be believed. The first is the smell – it honks like rotten eggs, thanks to sulphur being a by-product of the chemical reaction. Some more recent concoctions attempt to mask the odour with other smells, while others use chemical trickery to reduce the impact, but the odourless fallout remover currently only exists in detailers' night-time fantasies. The second is the colour, as when reacting with iron particles, the solution turns a vivid purple, which is why they are often called 'bleeding' fallout removers.

Top Tip

Manufacturers know that customers will believe their products are more effective if they change colour quickly and dramatically, so some have added ingredients which accelerate the colour change, regardless of whether or not they are reacting with iron – don't fall for it!

SPECIFIC CONTAMINANT REMOVAL

The washing and decontaminating processes so far have all been targeting 'normal' circumstances, but we regularly come across vehicles that have suffered a specific form of contamination that demands a targeted removal strategy. With all contamination, responding quickly will make removal easier and reduce the chances of permanent damage. Do not leave bird mess until the weather improves, or you have more time – it should be your top priority, alongside a regular brew and remembering to breathe.

The following table covers the most common issues car owners face, and possible solutions – starting with the safest option. These solutions are based on a modern car with clear coat – if you have an older car with cellulose paint, some solutions are not suitable. All these solutions are for when a car has already been washed and the contamination persists – in many cases a good safe wash will either lessen or remove contamination with little more than water and detergent.

Contamination	Solution 1	Solution 2	Solution 3
Bird lime (see opposite)	APC sprayed on, then jet off	Wet microfibre on mark, leave for 5 - 10 minutes, jet off, repeat	
Concrete	Mild acid wash, either acidic shampoo or added vinegar	Specialist product, e.g. Autosmart Congo	
Water-based paint spots	All-purpose cleaner,	Solvent cleaner, such as a panel wipe	Clay bar with plenty of lubricant
Oil-based paint spots	Steam cleaning	Tar & glue remover	Graffiti remover or clay bar
Sticker residue	Tar & Glue remover	Steam	Toffee wheel
Organic growth – e.g. moss	APC soak, agitation by brush, flushed with water.	Enzyme cleaner, e.g. Valet Pro or Autosmart Biobrisk	
Tree sap and honey dew*	APC with agitation and rinse	Tar remover	Turpentine or alcohol
Insect carcasses	APC soak and jet off	Dedicated insect remover	Traffic film remover
Water spotting	Acidic quick detailer	Water spot remover	Machine polishing

* Some types of tree sap require alternative approaches.

1 Some types of bird mess are more acidic than others, but all need removing swiftly.

2 First, soften the bird mess by laying a microfibre soaked in hot water over the mark.

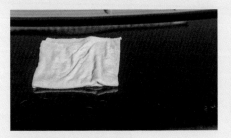

3 Leave the microfibre there for at least five minutes.

4 Carefully lift the microfibre so as not to abrade the paint surface.

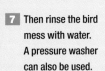

5 You can spray the bird mess with APC to start to break it down chemically.

6 Alternatively, you can use a pump spray to create a foam – in both cases, leave to dwell for a couple of minutes.

7 Then rinse the bird mess with water. A pressure washer can also be used.

8 In extreme circumstances, you may need to pinch it off with a clean microfibre.

Chapter 4

THE PAINT POLISHING PROCESS

Detailing is just another way of saying 'paint correction', right?

Wrong!

There is so much more to detailing than just polishing paint, but it is fair to say that paint correction is an essential skill for any detailer. Just don't fall into the trap of only learning how to polish, declaring yourself a detailer and neglecting to learn all of the other skills expected of a 'vehicle appearance specialist'.

PAINT TYPES

Automotive paint has evolved and changed as new technology becomes available and new demands are put upon it. The car has evolved from the horse-drawn carriage; early cars were painted in the same way as their predecessors using linseed oil mixed with pigment, which required days to air dry. This didn't suit the mass production techniques famously developed by Henry Ford, so people started to bake the paint at around 200 degrees, and formulated additives such as iron and lead to accelerate the drying process.

In the early 1920s, DuPont invented nitrocellulose paint. This could be applied using the newly developed spray gun, enabling easy application of multiple, thinner layers of paint and dramatically reducing drying time. The weakness of nitrocellulose paint was the susceptibility to solvents – petrol, for example, would make the paint fade and lose gloss.

⬇ Paint fade is common on older and red cars.

The 1930s saw the introduction of oil-based enamels, which were more durable, while the 1960s fostered water-based, acrylic enamels that had the added advantage of broadening the available colour palette from mostly black to all the colours of the rainbow. This is also when metallic particles were blended into paint for added sparkle.

All of these paints are collectively referred to as single-stage paint, cellulose, or 'celly' as a colloquial term. A common weakness is their susceptibility to UV damage, causing colours to fade through oxidation – red going pink, yellow becoming pale, and darker colours losing gloss and getting lighter.

In the late 1970s we saw the introduction of lacquer for automotive application – an additional clear layer applied on top of the colour or 'base coat'. These lacquers added gloss, but more importantly, contained UV filters that made the finish much more resistant to fading. Early iterations were limited to expensive cars and used isocyanate as a solvent in both the base and lacquer layers, which is terribly toxic for both the environment and the people using it. These are known as 2K or 2-pack paints and are still used today, particularly in the aftermarket.

The 1990s brought in water-based paints – the lacquer was still solvent-based, but the level of isocyanate used in total was reduced. While good news for both the environment and paint sprayers, the drying process was lengthened, and energy usage rose dramatically as the cars had to be baked twice to dry.

⬆ Paint transfer is normal on single-stage paints.

Modern cars are now painted with a variety of systems, both solvent- and water-based, with almost all vehicles having a base colour layer and lacquer applied on top. Manufacturers have steadily managed to make the process and result more efficient, with thinner, harder layers to save weight, cost and raw material.

Top Tip

When polishing your car, you shouldn't usually get any colour transfer onto your polishing pad, but if you do, don't panic – your car is likely painted with cellulose or enamel paint. If it isn't single-stage paint, then you may well want to start panicking.

PAINT THICKNESS GAUGES

When polishing paint, you are essentially removing clear coat or lacquer from the surface: you need to know how much clear coat is present so you don't 'burn through' it. Should you burn through the clear coat, your only option will be to add paint, either at a body shop or with a Small to Medium Area Repair Technique (SMART) service.

⬆ Ultrasonic PTGs can cost over £2,000.

Detailers use a combination of experience, judgement and paint thickness gauges (PTG) to judge how far they can go.

Paint thickness is measured in microns, and generally speaking, new cars leave the factory with between 120 and 160 microns of paint. Some Japanese manufacturers have got their paint process so refined that cars emerge with as little as 100 microns, while some luxury European brands apply over 250 microns to their products.

Within that paint depth are three layers – primer, base coat and lacquer – usually making up about a third of the overall depth each, though this is very much a rule of thumb. On a new vehicle with 120 microns of paint, one can usually assume that it has at least 30 microns of lacquer, as long as it hasn't been resprayed.

⬇ Typical clear coat (left) and single-stage paint (right) topography on a panel.

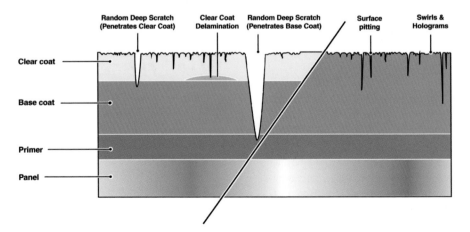

Clear coat paint   Single stage paint

Random Deep Scratch (Penetrates Clear Coat)

Clear Coat Delamination

Random Deep Scratch (Penetrates Base Coat)

Surface pitting

Swirls & Holograms

Clear coat

Base coat

Primer

Panel

The total depth of paint is not consistent between cars, panels or even parts of panels. Equally, cars often have body repairs – even between the factory and being delivered to the showroom – so you might find an average reading of 120 microns with an area presenting over 200 microns. Be very cautious in this situation because paint applied as part of a repair is often different and more delicate than factory-applied paint. Also, remember that those 200 microns are unlikely to be evenly distributed between just three layers – in fact, there may well be much less clear coat on the top layer than on the rest of the car.

Paint thickness gauges (PTGs) vary enormously in cost, reliability of reading, technology and resolution. Budget-conscious buyers can find PTGs for under £100 that use electromagnetic induction to establish the total depth of paint on ferrous surfaces. They are, however, easily thrown off by metallic paint and should only really be used as a rough guide or to spot previous repairs and resprays.

Mid-range models incorporate a secondary measurement system using eddy current, which monitors the frequency of a signal as it bounces back through a coating. This allows it to measure non-ferrous materials such as aluminium, and by using two measurement systems, can often give a more reliable reading. Though perfectly adequate for the home detailer, it is still wise to operate with at least a 10% error margin to be safe, and they won't work on composites like fibre glass and carbon fibre.

The most expensive options are in excess of £2,000 and use ultrasonic technology. This can measure the individual layers of paint on ferrous, non-ferrous and non-metallic surfaces, and can tell you how much clear coat is on a panel. However, while the total thickness reading will likely be as accurate as non-destructive testing can get, the reading for each layer should again only be used as a guide.

Almost all PTGs are used in the same way, with a probe mounted on the bottom of the device or attached by a short wire. The probe should be placed on the surface of the paint, perpendicular to it and a reading is displayed on the screen. Higher end models can remember hundreds of readings and output them to a computer. However, it is sensible to note down the readings with a simple diagram of where they were taken on a car.

For a professional, on a typical door, one would take six or seven evenly spaced readings, with perhaps some extra readings towards the edges and around features like door handles.

For the home user with a relatively simple device, it can be used more as a 'repair detector', where you take as many readings but only note down areas that stand out for being particularly high or low - then you know which areas to be particularly careful around.

If you don't have a PTG, there are still measures you can take to reduce the chances of accidentally burning through a repaired panel, such as examining each panel with a lamp to see changes in colour shade or orange peel texture, which allude to retro-applied paint. Pay attention to areas that are more likely to suffer damage – corners from parking scuffs, bonnets from stone chips, doors from car park dings, etc.

PAINT DEFECT GLOSSARY

We polish paint to remove imperfections, so it makes sense to look at some of the common paint defects, their causes, and possible steps that can be taken to rectify them.

Defect	Description
Swirl marks	Look like multiple circular scratches that dull the surface - actually lots of straight lines
Holograms	Visible in direct light, look like long wavy lines which shift according to viewpoint
Marring	Shallow scratches, usually grouped in straight, parallel lines. Can appear milky and dull (clay bar marring pictured overleaf)
Pigtails	Defined spiral scratches that overlap each other to form a 'texture'
DA haze	Very fine flecks that appear to be arranged in circles, often only viewable in certain lights
Random deep scratches	Isolated deep scratches, usually with a white tinge, not corrected with basic polishing
Orange peel	Literally like the surface of an orange peel – varying in severity
Sanding marks	Normally tightly packed straight-line scratches; if rounded and smooth, they could be under the paint, either in primer or filler, and not removable
Overspray	Spots that stand proud of the surface, often a different colour to the rest of the car
Etching	Looks like sticker residue, can usually be felt on the fingertip. Often circular but uneven
Stone chips	Small 'holes' in the paint, often through the clear and base coat, often appear white
Road rash	A collection of very small paint chips, common behind, and on the rear edge of wheel arches
Fisheyes	Circular dimples or indentations in the paint
Solvent pop	Small pinholes in the paint, often standing proud of the surface, or as little craters
Crazing	Spider webbing of cracks in the top layer of paint
Clear coat failure	Looks like a white translucent flaking of paint

Pig Tails

Swirl marks

Deeper scratches

Cause	Solution
Usually caused by poor washing and drying methods	Medium machine polishing, sometimes heavy polishing required
The result of rotary machine polishing that hasn't been finished or refined	Light machine polishing with a DA or rotary
The result of light abrasion, often from incorrect wash and decontamination methods	Light machine polishing
Caused by grit getting trapped in the pad on a DA polishing machine, or RO sanding	Depending on depth, they can be removed with wet sanding and/or machine polishing
The result of dual action machine polishing that hasn't been finished or refined	Light machine polishing with a clean pad and rotary machine
Multiple causes from vandalism to minor accidents – often caused by keys or watches	Sometimes require paint, often require wet sanding, sometimes can be fixed with heavy polishing
More of an attribute than a flaw, related to the painting process	Wet sanding can usually reduce the appearance but can rarely remove it entirely
Poor refinishing by a body shop or detailer. If under the paint: poor prep by body shop with filler sink	Wet sanding and polishing can normally reduce surface sanding marks. Sub-surface requires paint
The result of a car being parked near to where paint is being sprayed	Clay bar or tar remover (not together), denibbing tool, followed by light machine polishing
Regularly caused by acidic bird lime or alkaline mineral deposits in water, or other chemical damage	Can require paint, can sometimes be fixed with a heat gun, often polishing will work
Normally caused by stones being flung up by passing or leading vehicles	Touch-up paint followed by wet sanding and/or polishing
As per stone chips, but often caused by little stones flung up by your own wheels	Touch-up paint, often applied by spray gun or airbrush, followed by polishing
Often caused by oil, water or silicone contamination during painting	Body shop – beyond the scope of a detailer
Usually caused by poor painting technique with upper layers drying before lower layers	Body shop – even if some methods can reduce the visual impact short term
Caused by old age, poor application or poorly blended lacquer	Body shop – beyond the scope of a detailer
High exposure to UV light without protection	Body shop – beyond the scope of a detailer

1 Clay bar marring creates a milky appearance.

2 Wash marring and swirl marks can be removed by machine polishing.

3 The visual difference paint correction makes can be astounding.

4 Holograms can be inflicted with poor machine polishing techniques.

5 Swirl marks caused by a poor wash technique.

6 Scratches around door handles are common.

POLISHING MACHINES

There are hundreds of models of polishing machines on the market, to the point where it can be quite bewildering to choose between them. Professional detailers will have a range of machines in their arsenal to suit different tasks, whereas the enthusiast may be limited to one or two machines that can perform a range of roles to a reasonable standard.

The three key attributes that we will use to categorise the machines available are:

- **Movement type:** rotary / free-spinning Dual Action / forced-rotation Dual Action / selectable.
- **Power source:** corded / cordless / air-driven.
- **Size:** full-size / mini / micro.

⬇ There are polishing machines to suit all budgets.

Movement Types

Humans have been polishing surfaces to make them shiny for centuries, and as with most things, we have developed tools to make the process easier and more efficient as technology allows. When it comes to polishing cars, rotary machines were first on the block, derived from electric angle grinders, while dual action (DA) machines evolved from air-powered DA sanders, as did their forced-rotation brethren.

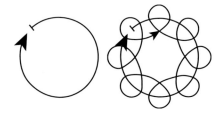

⬆ Rotary machines (left) rotate in a single axis that cannot be stalled without forcing the motor itself to stop as there is no clutch. DA machines (right) oscillate, with a secondary rotation, either passive (normal DA) or with a direct drive (forced rotation DA).

Rotary polishers are perhaps the easiest to understand, but the hardest to master, which is why most enthusiasts start with a DA. The rotary spins the pad on a single axis, there is no oscillation, and they are what we call direct-drive – there is no clutch between the motor and the pad. Conversely, the free-spinning DA moves the pad in oval orbits without actively spinning it – the rotation is a secondary effect of the oscillation and can be stopped, or 'stalled', when excess pressure is applied. The forced-rotation DA is a lovechild of both machines, which uses a planetary gear to rotate the pad as it orbits.

DA machines are generally classified by the size of their throw – how far the pad is thrown off centre. On small machines and sanders this can be as low as 3mm, and on full-size alternatives 21mm is about the most you will see in automotive detailing.

➡ Some machines can have more than one movement type that you can switch between.

⬇ DA machines like these are generally easier to use than rotary alternatives.

We now also see multi-movement machines, such as the LC Power Tools UDOS 51E. These allow users to switch between a rotary movement and four different DA movements. Makita's PO500C can be used as both a free-spinning DA and a forced-rotation DA. Nano-style small area polishers (bottom right) also have manually interchangeable heads for convenience and versatility.

Power sources

Most polishing machines on the market are mains-powered, but as lithium battery and brushless motor technologies improve and become more affordable, many manufacturers are offering cordless alternatives. There are benefits and weaknesses to both options: corded machines don't run out of battery and can ultimately supply more torque. However, cordless machines do away with the pesky cable, increasing safety, ease of use and flexibility in terms of where you can polish your car. Detailers tend to only use air-powered sanders – though some can be adapted for polishing duties, the relative cost of a hefty compressor, added noise and limited tool options don't make it an appealing option for the enthusiast.

⬆ Lithium batteries and brushless motors have revolutionised cordless polishers.

For a long time, 6mm was the standard until 'long-throw' 15mm and 21mm machines were developed. Generally speaking, the longer the throw, the faster a machine can correct paint with a given pad and compound combination. However, larger throws suit big, flat expanses of bodywork; not curvaceous and intricate areas where shorter throw machines thrive.

⬇ Air-driven machines are usually for sanding rather than polishing.

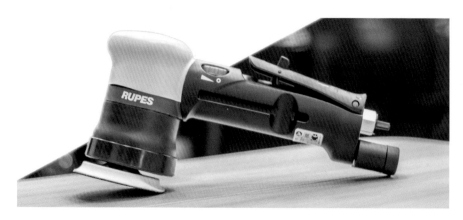

➡ Smaller machines are more suited to curved surfaces.

SIZE

Back in the 'olden days', there was pretty much one standard size of machine polisher – it was big, heavy, rotary, and it would be impossible to break. For more intricate areas, detailers would improvise, using extension bars and home-punched pads to get into door-handle recesses and the like. Thankfully, manufacturers now offer a plethora of products to cater for every requirement, from hefty rotaries that can use vast wool 'bonnets' like the Flex PE14-1 180 right down to delicate little devices like the Rupes iBrid Nano, affectionately known as the 'electric toothbrush' among detailers. For the enthusiast, a smaller machine is easier to handle and while it takes longer to correct a given area, when you're doing it for pleasure, efficiency isn't the top priority.

WHICH MACHINE?

Ask just about any detailer what their first machine polisher was and they will say a 6mm DA such as a Porter Cable or DAS6, unless they are chronologically enhanced, in which case it will likely be a rotary machine. As one of the most popular models, the DAS6 is not just a machine, it is an institution, helping tens of thousands of car care enthusiasts to get into machine polishing. It is also not a single machine – the original design has been developed and upgraded over the years and branded by at least a dozen different companies, with 'Pro' versions offering more power, 'Plus' versions offering a longer throw and 'v2' and 'v3' versions offering a more refined driveline and other upgrades.

⬇ Micro polishers like the Rupes Nano iBrid (left) and Flex PXE (right) can be useful.

⬆ After the DAS6, people often progress onto long-throw DAs, such as the Rupes LHR15.

For those who have perhaps already gone through their 'DAS6' phase and are looking to get into more serious machinery, the next step would be a long-throw DA, usually something offering 15mm of oscillation. With all machine genres, there is a big price spectrum between the cheapest and most expensive, despite visual similarities and comparable on-paper specifications. The differences between the dearest and most affordable are normally only noticeable after long-term ownership – more expensive options are often smoother and built to a higher standard – so suit the professional and regular users better.

For those who feel they have mastered the long-throw DA and are wanting to push further, the next step would either be a forced-rotation DA or a full-blown rotary. For the former there are offerings from Makita, Vertool, Rupes, and Flex, among others, depending on how deep your pockets are. For rotary machines, there are even more options, some starting under £100. At this point in your experience you will be in a position where you know what you're looking for and what feels right for you – and there is no correct answer we can offer, just a suggestion to try as many machines as you can and go with whichever option you 'click' with. You can often try multiple machines while on training courses, or at detailing shows and events.

⬇ The trusty DAS6 is where many detailers started.

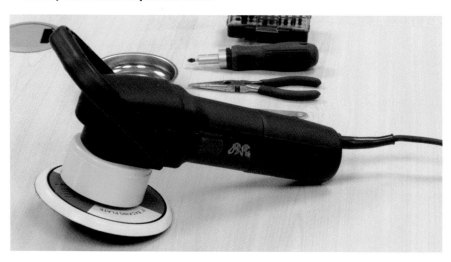

POLISHING PADS

Part of becoming a proficient detailer is understanding pads, the different types and how to get the best from them. Most pads are constructed of wool, foam or microfibre, and within these categories there are many variations that we will also look at. Other materials, such as denim, have been used in the past, but these three media are all you will ever need to detail a car. Pads come in many different diameters, thicknesses and surface textures, creating innumerable combinations of pad, compound and machine.

↟ Originally, pads were wool, and wool pads still have their place today.

↟ The same compound on alternative pads can behave very differently.

Wool pads

Wool pads predate their foam counterparts, and while they have a reputation for being primarily for heavy correction work, you can use them in a multitude of roles, including finishing. Traditionally they have been for rotary use only, but now manufacturers have developed shorter-haired versions for DA use too, while their common advantage over foam is that they generate less heat during use.

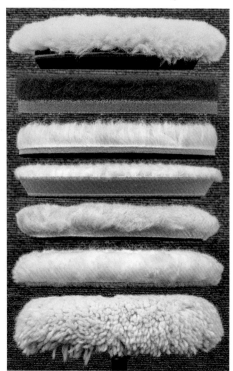

Within the 'wool' genre you get fine and coarse, long and short, straight and twisted strands, natural and synthetic, and even blends of different 'wool' on the same pad. Some manufacturers have even created 'foamed wool', a process designed to provide the benefits of both media without their respective drawbacks.

Foam pads

Foam pads are just as multifarious, ranging from aggressive cutting pads to super-soft alternatives designed to be used in the finishing stages. They can be used with both rotary and DA machines, and are available in dozens of different sizes and thicknesses. Most foam polishing pads are what we call 'open-cell', and their aggressiveness is controlled by the size of these cells – smaller, densely packed cells make softer pads, larger cells make more aggressive cutting pads. Some foams have a consistent density through their thickness, with just a Velcro disc attached to their rear, while others have a denser, stiffer layer of foam at the rear to give more rigidity overall.

You will find many foam pads have textures on their top surface – some have egg-crate style bumps, some have parallel fins, some have hexagonal shapes cut into them, some even have holes right through them. It could be argued that this is for better thermal performance, preventing hotspots appearing on the surface or within the pad, while cynics may say that it is purely for manufacturers to distinguish their product from their competitors.

You will also see pads with different edge profiles, including chamfered, straight and bevelled. Various reasons are given for a particular profile, some offering better visibility for the detailer, some claiming better thermal management and others claiming their design is easier to use. Ultimately it boils down to personal preference – learning which sort of pads work best for you in each situation is part of the process of building your experience.

⬆ Temperature control is a very important part of machine polishing.

Top Tip

Thermal management is a major part of machine polishing. Polishing works through friction, which produces heat. Some heat is useful for breaking down compounds; too much heat is very destructive for both paint and pad. Pad design, construction, and machine type play a role in how much heat is produced, but the biggest factor is methodology – using too much pressure and failing to keep the polisher moving will cause excess heat; running the machine too fast will have a similar effect. Also consider the material you are polishing: metal conducts heat away from the area being polished to the rest of the panel quite efficiently; however, plastic is an insulator so is more susceptible to hot spots.

Manufacturers also make their pads in different colours; the idea being that this makes them easily identifiable when you are looking for a certain cutting pad or finishing pad. These colours often correspond to polishes and compounds that have appropriately coloured packaging and labels. In theory this is a great system. However, different manufacturers use different colour systems which can be confusing if – like most detailers – you use a range of pads and compounds from more than one manufacturer. Also, it can mislead people into thinking you *have* to use compound X with pad Y and you *have* to use an aggressive cutting compound with an aggressive pad, when in fact there are plenty of occasions when you might use a fine compound with a medium pad, for example.

Microfibre pads

Microfibre pads are a relatively new development, introduced by Meguiar's around 2010, and have since been widely adopted by detailers worldwide, with other manufacturers developing their own versions.

↑ Microfibre pads can offer higher rates of correction than foam alternatives.

One major limitation of free-spinning DA machines was the lack of cutting power they provided compared to rotary machines, particularly rotary machines used in conjunction with wool pads, which were unsuitable for DAs at the time. Microfibre pads went a long way to solving this problem, offering more cut than foam while also being well suited to use with a DA – in fact they are responsible, at least in part, for DAs becoming so popular and opening up 'detailing' to the enthusiast audience. Microfibre pads are harder to clean than foam and ultimately don't finish as well, so they are not a perfect solution that makes foam and wool obsolete, but for both experienced and novice DA users they are a very useful addition to the armoury.

Backing plates

Between the machine and the pad you have something called a backing plate, and just in case you felt there weren't enough variations between pad and machine, these backing plates can add another variable. Ultimately, their role

⬇ Backing plates come in different shapes and sizes for different machines.

↑ The thickness of a backing plate influences what it is like to use.

is to transfer torque from the machine to the pad, but they also provide flexibility, pad compatibility, pressure distribution, vibration suppression and heat absorption.

As with pad and compound choice, there is no such thing as 'the best' backing plate. However there are going to be backing plates that suit your polishing style and pad choice better than others. Not all packing plates are compatible with all polishing machines, for example a backing plate designed for a rotary will not fit a dual action machine, so research fitment prior to purchase.

The best way to find the right combination for you is to start with what a manufacturer supplies or recommends and then experiment with different options as you gain more experience.

⬇ Some backing plates have holes for cooling the pad.

↑ Thicker and softer backing plates make it easier for pads to curve to the shape of the panel.

⬇ Thinner and harder backing plates can give the user a better sense of control and precision.

POLISHING COMPOUNDS

The terms 'compound' and 'polish' are often used interchangeably to describe a liquid or paste applied to the polishing pad to assist with abrasion and lubrication. There is no real distinction between the two, though 'compound' generally alludes to the coarser end of the spectrum and polish to the finer end. In simple terms, the difference between compounds is how aggressive they are – the more aggressive they are, the faster they will correct paint; the finer they are, the better the finish they will provide. You start with an aggressive compound and repeat the process with ever finer compounds to achieve the desired finish, much like you would with sandpaper on wood.

Except, as you've probably guessed by now, it really isn't that simple.

⬆ There are literally hundreds of compounds to try from all over the world, most are designed to work as part of a system on specific pads and machines.

➡ Heavy cut compound on a wool pad via a rotary machine is likely to cut quickly.

The first major distinction is between SMAT and DAT polishes. Super Micro Abrasive Technology (SMAT) has been around for a long time, but just as the DAS6 and microfibre pads revolutionised their little niche, Diminishing Abrasive Technology (DAT) has had a significant impact on the world of compounds. SMAT compounds remain at a fixed level of abrasion during use and are more common in the coarser ranges. DAT polishes start at a certain level of cut and then break down in a linear manner so that after they have been worked, they provide a finer level of cut. There are coarse DAT polishes, but most start in the medium range and work down to the fine or super-fine range. The idea behind DAT polishes is that you don't need as many stages to take paint from badly swirled to concours-ready.

➡ When maginfied 400x this is what a SMAT medium cut compound looks like.

⬇ Manufacturers use colour-coded pads and compounds, but it showed only be viewed as a guide, they can work when mixed up.

Many believe that the compound is doing all the work when it comes to paint correction, when in fact the pad is doing a lot of the abrasion, and the compound is acting as a lubricant between the pad and the paint. Consequently, the quality of a compound isn't just down to how well it cuts, but also how well it works with the pad, how much dust and heat it produces and how long it can be worked before drying out.

The level of cut provided by a compound is usually referenced in its name; either with a term such as 'coarse' or 'fine' to describe the physical attributes, or as 'heavy cut' and 'finishing' to describe its application, or as a number to reflect the type of sanding marks it can remove, with lower numbers representing coarser polish. You also get 'one-step' compounds, essentially DAT polishes that will correct and refine to a finish in 'one step'. These aren't to be mistaken with 'All In One' or 'AIO' polishes, which are normally fine DAT polishes that also contain a glazing agent to correct, refine and protect paint with one product. However, as mentioned, the real-world level of cut provided by a compound is dependant on pad and machine choice, as well as how they are used, and the paint being polished.

You will often hear detailers mention 'fillers' in reference to compounds, with

← Perhaps the most famous all-in-one is Autoglym Super Resin Polish, launched in 1986.

⬇ Panel wipes and paint cleansers are often referred to as 'truth serum' by detailers.

the general attitude that they are a bad thing. If you imagine the surface of perfect paint to be completely flat, then consider imperfect paint to have a rough surface with peaks and troughs, and the purpose of polishing is to wear down the peaks to be the same height as the troughs, and thus return to a perfectly smooth surface. Fillers take the opposite approach and instead of reducing the peaks, they fill the troughs, thus providing that perfect surface. The problem is that these fillers are not permanent – eventually they will wash out and reveal the troughs that they have been masking.

Some products rely on fillers – most notably glazes – while organic waxes have a filling effect that allows lightly swirled paint to look much better temporarily. However, some compounds contain fillers to give the impression of perfect paint even though they haven't abraded the peaks away completely.

Compounds like AIOs are 'allowed' to do this because they don't masquerade as products that will correct paint entirely. However, conventional compounds that contain fillers are maligned by detailers as they can give the impression a panel has been corrected to a high standard, only to drop back within days to reveal the swirls they have been masking.

All compounds contain oils and lubricants to work, and these also have a filling effect, so it is essential to use a specific paint cleanser between polishing steps to reveal the true condition of the paint. Panel wipe is colloquially referred to as 'truth serum' by detailers, which we will explore in more detail shortly.

Picking your combination

The chart below explains the parameters that need to be considered and the choices to be made when machine polishing.

Consider	Experiment	Adjust
Variables which will affect your choice of products include:	**Variables which you can adjust to alter the performance include:**	
Paint Type →	Pad Choice →	
Paint Depth →	Machine Choice →	Not every panel will react the same, so continue to test and adjust as needed
Paint Defects →	Compound Choice →	
Substrate →	Stages →	
Desired Finish →	Machine Speed →	
Time available →	Arm Speed →	
Kit available →	Pressure →	
Skill Level →	Pad Size →	

PRINCIPLES OF MACHINE POLISHING

Learning how to polish paint cannot be achieved by reading a book or watching a video. It is a hands-on skill that needs to be practised and refined over many hundreds of hours. However, we can guide you through the processes involved in theory, so that you can start to put them into practice in the real world.

We would strongly recommend getting some scrap bonnets from your local car breakers to practice on before

⬇ Most matte and satin finishes are vinyl wraps, but not all are, neither should ever be polished.

putting pad to paint on a real car, even your own. Equally, if you start out with a free-spinning DA, foam pads and relatively fine polishes, you're much less likely to cause damage than if you crack out a full-size rotary with a wool pad and heavy-cut compound.

Top Tip

Never polish matte or satin finishes on paint or vinyl. By smoothing the surface you will add gloss and destroy the finish irreparably.

Preparation

Once you have washed, decontaminated, dried and taken paint depth readings, you're nearly ready to start polishing. While it is possible to machine polish a car outside, if you have access to some space under cover, it will be much easier to control environmental variables such as light, temperature and humidity. Working inside also keeps you away from wind and rain, neither of which are conducive to an enjoyable polishing session.

Find a space that gives you a good metre free all around the car, ideally a bit more so you can fit a trolley behind you to hold the essentials: keeping pads, machines, tea, compounds and even lighting rigs close to you for easy access. Professional detailers often use scissor lifts too, allowing the surface they are polishing

⬆ The more comfortable it is to work, the less risk there is of harming yourself.

to be at a more comfortable height to work with. For detailers, these are better than conventional two - and four-pillar - lifts as they get 360-degree access to the vehicle. If you are using a lift, ensure you do so safely on equipment rated for the weight of the vehicle.

Top Tip

It sounds daft, but make sure there is enough headroom for the vehicle before forcing your Range Rover through the roof of your garage. Also, if your car is equipped with air suspension, you may need to lock it in a specific mode prior to lifting - usually in a settings menu.

The next step is to tape up the car. Detailers use a variety of masking tapes to protect surfaces abutting where you are polishing from getting scuffed. This includes, but is not limited to, rubber and plastic trim, decals and keyholes, lights and panel edges. Masking also has the added benefit of stopping polish residue from becoming entrenched in crevices – you'll spend half the time taping up compared to how long it takes to tease dried compound from a window seal.

While normal masking tape will do, it can leave adhesive residue, which can be irritating to remove after polishing. Consequently, detailers tend to use 3M 3434 (blue) or 3030 (green) tape, among various other options. With different tapes

come different levels of tack, different widths, different characteristics in terms of flexibility, water resistance and heat resistance, as well as the amount of adhesive residue left behind – the choice is usually a subjective one.

Getting started
Having just read about the different machines, pads, polishes and backing plates, you're probably building up a mental shopping list of everything you'll need to get started, and considering how to explain to your partner that you need to remortgage the house. There is no need. In these formative stages you just need a free-spinning DA, a small selection of foam pads (many of which are often included with the polishing machine itself), along with the backing plate and a compound or two to get started.

⬇ Masking up around trim and panel edges reduces the chance of causing damage.

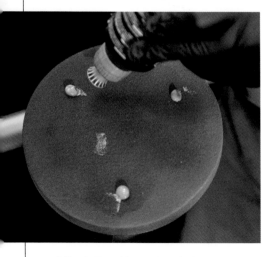

↑ You don't want too much product on your polishing pad.

↓ Be sure to spread the compound as much as possible.

We'd recommend a medium DAT polish and then a finishing DAT polish, which will allow you to make a significant improvement to a typical car while minimising the risks of damaging it. You won't get deeper marks out and you certainly won't be able to remove orange peel, but you will remove marring caused by clay bars and imperfect wash methods, and you'll be able to add a ton of gloss in so doing.

Make sure your pad is located properly onto the backing plate – if it is off-centre you will get added vibration. Squeeze out three or four pea-sized blobs of polish directly onto the pad. Using a gloved finger, ideally one of your own, spread the compound evenly over the surface of the pad – this is called priming the pad and ensures compound is not immediately absorbed into the pad rather than sitting on top of it. Repeat the process of adding four pea-sized blobs to the pad, then gently place the pad onto the paint at evenly spaced spots within an area of about 80cm² - around half a newspaper page - leaving compound on the surface of the paint. The area that you can polish in one set is dependent upon experience, arm length, the compound and machine you are using, and the nature of the panel – large flat surfaces are easier than intricate ones. As ever, start small and gradually build up as you feel comfortable, and try not to expand beyond what is within arms reach.

Then, without adding any more compound, place the pad on the paint and start the machine on its lowest speed setting. Do not apply any pressure, just let the weight of the machine itself keep the pad and paint in contact. Move the machine in straight, methodical lines around the designated zone to be polished, creating a fine film of compound. In theory, the hand holding the rear of the machine by the cable is doing most of the work and your other hand is merely guiding the head of the machine.

Once there is an even coat of compound, you can increase the speed of the machine, but keep it moving in straight, overlapping lines and go back over the 80cm^2 area. Depending on the polish, pad and pressure being applied, you may need to do anything from three to seven 'passes' over the same area to fully work the polish. The idea is that you are breaking down the DAT polish with a combination of heat and friction. If you don't work the polish for long enough, the finish won't be as good as it could be; if you work it for too long, the polish will dry out and you will start making the finish worse. Depending on the polish, you can usually tell when to stop – the compound will go clear and the machine will start to 'grab'.

Top Tip

Detailers use three terms when it comes to polishing, and it is really important to know the differences between them: stage, step and pass. If someone says they have done a two-**stage** polish on a vehicle, they mean they have done multiple steps and passes with two different pad and compound combinations. If someone says they have done two **steps** it means they have applied a compound and worked it through twice. If someone says they have done a two-**pass** polish, they have moved the polishing machine over the same area twice during the same step.

⬇ Holding the machine correctly and comfortably is really important for good results.

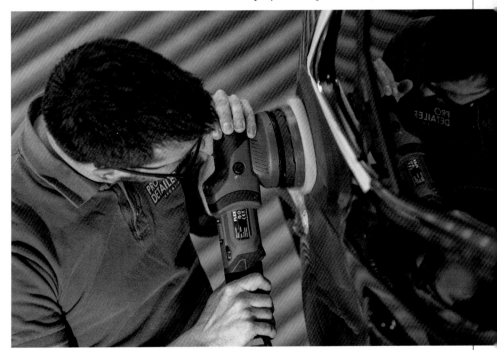

As you build confidence, you can start to add a little pressure to the machine. The benefit of using a DA is that if you add too much pressure, the pad will stall and stop rotating, at which point you can ease off. It really helps to use a black marker pen to add a line on the foam part of the backing plate – this makes it easier to see when the pad is spinning properly and when it has stalled. It is important to keep the pad flat to the paint; if you have it at an angle it won't have the desired effect and will stall with less pressure.

⬇ Built-for-purpose paint cleanser is better than just IPA.

Once you feel you have finished with the step, stop the machine while it is still in contact with the paint but with minimal pressure, even taking some of the weight of the machine itself. This reduces 'fling' – where compound is flung out of the spinning pad.

Take a clean, soft microfibre to gently buff the residue off, then spray some panel wipe onto it. Gently wipe the area you have just polished, wait 30 seconds or so, and turn the microfibre to wipe the area again with the clean side. This will remove any polish residue and reveal the true improvement your efforts have made on the paint. Look at the paint from different angles and hold a light to it to get a better view – from some angles you can hide defects entirely, often by accident, so check thoroughly.

Top Tip

Many think that just using an alcohol solution, usually IPA (isopropyl alcohol), is enough to remove all the residue left by polishing. This is not true. Proper panel wipes may indeed contain IPA, but they will also contain other solvents like petroleum naphtha, ethyl acetate and toluene that break down different types of residue. Even with panel wipe, some compounds contain acrylic fillers that can prove stubborn, though these are normally in one-step products designed to give maximum visual improvement with the minimum amount of effort. Be careful when using these products and take heed of all safety and personal protective equipment recommendations as they can be quite harmful.

Once you have become comfortable using a small DA and relatively light polishes, you can start to experiment with different pad, compound, machine and technique combinations. Whatever you do, don't rush into a wool pad on a rotary with flatting compound – becoming proficient at machine polishing takes hundreds of hours; to become an expert takes thousands.

Top Tip

It is important to clean pads after use and sometimes even during use. This can be done in various ways, from dedicated pad-washing buckets to a simple scrub with a brush. Compressed air can be very effective, while there are also various chemicals & tools available to assist.

Another variable to consider when building your experience is the difference between paints. Online you will see generalisations about certain cars, colours and paint types: 'paint on German cars is hard', 'paint on Japanese cars is

⬆ Cleaning pads is an essential process – dirty pads cause damage.

soft', 'that faded red paint will be single stage'. While these may often be true, never take what other people have said about other cars as gospel – the car in front of you may well defy all stereotypes, so work with what you know.

We would suggest getting a selection of panels from a range of different vehicles to practise on. Challenge yourself with, for example, a black bonnet from a mid-noughties' Japanese car, which *might* be difficult to get perfect. At the other end of the spectrum, a Mercedes with ceramic clearcoat (look for a 'C' at the beginning of the paint code) *may* be a challenge to correct before you even get to the refining stages. Modern cars are almost all painted by robots, which you might think would make the process consistent, but the fact remains that exactly the same make, model and colour of car, made at the same factory on the same day, might have different characteristics.

LIGHTING

Walk into any professional detailing bay and you will find a plethora of different lights: they are there for good reason. Before we had access to such a range of light sources, one would spend hours polishing a car under halogen or fluorescent lights. We would think the car was pretty much perfect until we wheeled it back out into the sunshine, at which point hearts would sink, tears would be shed and expletives would be uttered.

The problem with using a fixed, single source of direct light is that while it may reveal some defects, it will never show everything. Every artificial light source has what we call a 'correlated colour temperature' (CCT), measured in Kelvin (K), with warm, yellow light having a lower Kelvin value than cold, blue light. There is also Colour Rendering Index (CRI) to consider, which is a scale of the impact that a light has on the colour of the object it is lighting.

In an ideal world, you want to have lights that collectively cover the central half of the CCT spectrum, which normally involve having a combination of different types of light – halogens and incandescent make up the lower, warmer frequencies; LEDs generally produce the 'daylight' centre of the spectrum; with fluorescent tubes offering higher, more blue-tinted hues. Lighting technology has come a long way, and LED has led the charge, with manufacturers like Scangrip and Sealey producing multi-temperature lights with high CRI ratings above 95. These can switch between different temperatures (usually from around 2,500K up to around 6,500K), and have the added benefit of a

dimming facility, as too much light can wash out defects just as easily as too little light can hide them.

Another dimension of lighting is reflection angle and diffused versus direct light. In professional detailing bays you will see lights mounted at knee-height, head-height and on the ceiling, to ensure light is hitting the car from lots of different angles. You will also see detailers wielding handheld lights, which is again so they can manipulate the reflection to spot any defects. These handheld lights may look like torches, but as with their larger brethren, they are in fact highly advanced (and expensive) full-spectrum lights. Some detailing studios also have diffused lights, where they are either pointed at a white ceiling, rather than directly at a car, or behind a white sheet of material. This is to

create large, consistent sources of light rather than a bright spot from a diode or bulb filament.

You would imagine detailers want as much light as possible so would paint their walls gloss white, yet nowadays you will find most areas used for paint correction are matte grey (or at least the lower sections are), and the floor is often a lighter grey. This is to stop reflections from the vehicle and other light sources interfering with the view of the painted surface. Conversely, some studios will have white walls for areas where ceramic coatings and paint protection film (PPF) is applied – as high spots and other problems are easier to spot with more light.

So, now you're building a large studio with at least two bays and a plethora of different lights, the cost of the pads and

↑ Detailing bays can resemble sci-fi film sets.

the machines seem really quite reasonable…. Of course, you don't *have* to do this to polish your Ford Focus. Generally, a simple LED work light that puts out between 5,000K and 6,000K – ideally with a dimming function – is all you need. There are plenty of rechargeable, cordless models on the market for under £100, and they will be useful for other household tasks like finding a lost dog in the dark, changing a fuse during a storm, and burying the body of the neighbour who reversed into your Ford Focus. Equally, you can grab some matte grey paint from a hardware store and just do the lower sections of your garage wall if you want to create a talking point.

Chapter 5

THE PAINT PROTECTION PROCESS

Once you have spent a weekend polishing your car, the next step is to protect your work. Even if you haven't polished your car, adding a sacrificial layer will help extend its lifespan and potentially make it easier to clean.

Detailers refer to these as LSPs which stands for 'last stage products', 'last step products' or even 'last step protection' – no one really knows which. As you can imagine, there are thousands of LSPs out there, so we will divide them into four genres before getting into the gritty details.

WAX

Wax was the first form of paint protection and it predates the invention of the car, and indeed even the invention of car paint itself.

Wax is essentially a non-soluble solid substance that becomes liquid with heated and then becomes a solid again when cooled. Wax occurs in nature, but humans have learnt to modify it for preferential properties, and synthesise it entirely to the same end.

There are organic car waxes ('organic' wax refers to the wax content of a wax-based product – there are other ingredients such as solvents and carrier solutions that aren't always organic per se – you can't harvest wax and put it in a pot unprocessed) and what we call 'hybrid' waxes, which mix synthetic and organic ingredients.

⬆ Waxes have been around longer than the car though they were commoditised in the 1950s.

Wholly synthetic products come under the polymer sealant category, despite often being marketed as waxes. Most waxes are sold as a solid paste of varying hardness, but there are also 'liquid' emulsion waxes with a thick consistency and 'spray waxes', which are generally thinner.

⬆ Liquid waxes are often quicker to apply but generally contain less organic wax, so are usually synthetic hybrids.

⬇ More recent waxes blend organic and synthetic active ingredients, referred to as 'hybrid' waxes.

⬆ Dodo Juice Blue Velvet contains beeswax and Carnauba, it is a classic 'organic' wax.

⬆ Be careful not to over-apply wax. A thin film is sufficient.

Another sub-division regularly used in reference to waxes is based on the intended application. At one end of the spectrum you have 'show waxes', which are designed to give the ultimate gloss and 'wet-look' at the potential cost of durability. These are often quite soft paste waxes and are designed to be easy to apply. On the other end of the scale there are 'protection' waxes, which are all about long-term durability. These are often hard waxes that can take more effort to apply, and are more sensitive to the level of preparation done prior to application.

Top Tip

Wax and polish are NOT the same – a polish will alter the surface it is applied to, and may contain a 'wax' element, whereas a wax is designed purely to sit on top of a surface. When a non-detailer says they have given their car 'a polish' they have normally waxed it on a Saturday afternoon; when a detailer says they have given the car 'a good polish' they have normally slaved over the vehicle for days with compounds, pads and machines galore.

Other 'general-purpose' waxes strike a balance between gloss, longevity and ease of use. There are also specialist waxes, such as those designed for wheels, or those that are 'colour-charged' to enhance specific colours of paint.

Within the 'organic' category there are several different waxes that are used by manufacturers, each with their own strengths and weaknesses. Beeswax and paraffin wax are on the softer side, offering ease of use, hydrophobicity and in the latter case, an element of chemical resistance. Montan, Candelilla and famously Carnauba waxes are much harder and provide durability. A typical organic product will use a mixture of hard and soft wax to make a product that is usable but durable.

Be wary of manufacturers who claim to sell 100% Carnauba wax – if a product was literally Carnauba wax in a tin it would be unusable – essentially a brick. What manufacturers mean is that *100% of the wax in a product* is Carnauba wax, even if that product is only 5% wax.

Generally speaking, for a top-end hard wax, you very rarely find more than 30–35% Carnauba – but again the waters can be muddied by measuring wet weight as opposed to dry weight, or by assuming all residual solid content is wax.

The main benefits of organic waxes are ease of use, the warm gloss they provide, impressive beading and the sheer traditional joy of application. Organic wax relies on the 'joy of application', as its major weakness is its durability, meaning that one must reapply it regularly to maintain gloss and protection. This is where hybrid waxes come in, as they contain various synthetic elements – usually silicone-derived, to add longevity. A typical organic wax may last four to six weeks; a good hybrid wax can last four to six months.

POLYMER SEALANTS

Polymer sealants are essentially waxes, usually in liquid form, that are crafted by chemists, not nature. They use engineered polymer chains to bond to each other and the paint itself. This not only provides better adhesion to paint, but also tighter surface cohesion, resulting in better chemical resistance and a longer life than wax. While top-end products can be just as expensive as organic waxes, generally speaking they are more cost effective as they don't need to be applied as often, and the ingredients don't have to be sourced from slow-growing trees like the *Copernicia prunifera* tree, from which Carnauba is harvested. However, many would argue that the quality of the gloss created by a polymer lacks the depth and lustre of that created by its organic counterpart.

Polymer sealants come in many different forms, ranging from spray-on and rinse-off washcoats to thick emulsions akin to liquid waxes. You will find polymer sealant components in other products too, particularly those that claim to add protection as a bonus to their primary use – for example wash and wax shampoos, quick detailers and even All In One polishes. The best protection will come from dedicated protection products – if you enjoy using a hard wax consider Fusso Coat from Soft99, if you prefer a creamy liquid wax you could try Meguiar's Ultimate Liquid Wax, or if you prefer a simple spray-on, wipe-off consider CarPro Hydro2 – all are polymer sealants. We aren't including a guide as to how to apply polymer sealants because they vary

⬆ There is a huge range of polymer sealants on the market.

between products, so reading the label – ideally before you start applying the product – is the best advice we will give.

⬇ Soft99 Fusso looks like a wax but is, in fact, a polymer sealant.

NANO & CERAMIC SEALANTS

Nanotechnology started appearing in car care products at the turn of the millennium, with companies such as Gtechniq producing advanced products unlike the organic waxes and polymer sealants we had seen before. Though the term 'ceramic coating' wasn't in common parlance until after the first decade had elapsed, the technology, even in nascent form, has been with us since 2006.

Considered the most durable form of paint protection this side of PPF, ceramic coatings have been the hot topic of the previous decade. Initially they were aimed purely at the professional detailing market, as they were difficult to apply and required very specific conditions to work properly. While there are still professional-only products, the home user can access a

⬇ Ceramic sealants require much more care to apply properly.

whole plethora of coatings over the internet, which is both good and bad news.

The bad news is that there are plenty of coatings out there that are really tricky to apply for a typical home user, and if they go wrong, can be very difficult to rectify. Equally, there are many products that are being imported under the radar that contain a high concentration of volatile organic compounds (VOCs) and very little in the way of health and safety information. These are positively dangerous, and we implore you to select your products with care from recognised manufacturers through official channels.

The good news is that as a diligent home enthusiast, you now have access to chemicals with the sort of technology your predecessors could only dream of. A legitimate ceramic coating, when correctly applied to properly prepared paint, can provide a durable, hydrophobic protective layer that can last years.

As with polymer sealants, each ceramic coating will have its own guidelines for use, and we would suggest following those. In principle, one applies the product to a microsuede cloth wrapped around a foam applicator, and this is applied to the vehicle in straight, overlapping lines, section by section. Some products require buffing off within a couple of minutes, others allow you longer so you can go around the whole car, rather than panel-by-panel. Most coatings need several hours to dry and several days to cure, so are best applied in a garage when the vehicle isn't needed for at least a day or two. Some professional products even require infrared (IR) curing lamps to work properly.

⬆ Many ceramic coatings are best left to the professionals.

The ceramic polemic

Log on to any detailing forum or online group and you will find a melée of dispute and debate regarding nano and so-called 'ceramic' products. To try and provide some clarity through the smoke and mirrors of marketing departments and keyboard-equipped quasi-chemists, we will go back to basics...

➡ When cured, ceramic coatings look like broken glass.

↑ Angelwax Enigma was among the first waxes to use properly blended SiO_2 to enhance its performance.

↑ Spray sealants can be quick, easy to apply and relatively durable.

'Nano' is referencing a nanometre, one millionth of a millimetre. In this context it is used to refer to the size of molecule in a given product. The concept being that by engineering a product on such a minute scale, you are creating a more advanced product that will offer superior performance – think 4K video vs SD. The 'nano' component normally refers to polysilanes, polysiloxanes and polysilazanes used in a formulation, which are truly advanced and offer resistance, slickness and hardness that a wax can't hope to compete with.

'Ceramic' is an even more contentious term which, outside of detailing, would normally refer to clay pots or exhaust heat shield coatings. In detailing it is often used interchangeably with 'SiO_2' – the abbreviation of silicon dioxide, known as quartz to geologists. Initially this gave rise to 'ceramic coatings', 'quartz coatings' and 'glass coatings' (SiO_2 is a major constituent of sand, which in turn is used to make glass), and now just about every genre of car care product has had the

marketing makeover to claim a ceramic constituent.

In some forms, SiO_2 does offer advantageous properties – for waxes it can add to the filling properties; for sealant coatings it can add hardness and slickness – but both rely on it being integrated into the chemistry of a product at a fundamental level. However, you *can* purchase SiO_2 cheaply in powder form, which is often used to lubricate wires within a multi-core cable, and can be sprinkled into just about anything you like. It will make no improvement to the performance of the product but you can truthfully say it is an SiO_2-containing potion on the label.

It is very easy to fall down the rabbit hole on the topic of ceramic products and end up lost and confused. For many home enthusiasts, waxes and polymer sealants will more than satisfy the desire for gloss and beading, and there are plenty of easy-to-use spray sealants that use very similar nano technology to 'proper' coatings with far less hassle, such as Gtechniq C2 v3 and Dodo Juice Future Armour.

PAINT PROTECTION FILM

Paint protection film (PPF) is perhaps the ultimate in paint protection and is even applied to parts of some vehicles at the factory. Think of it like a thick clear film that is precisely cut to shape and applied to a car with a removable adhesive. Being plastic, many are 'self-healing', where judicious use of heat can 'flow' out small scratches and scuffs.

Trying to PPF an entire car at home is perhaps a fool's errand when there are plenty of professionals who already have all the equipment and expertise needed.

However, if you fancy turning your hand to it, why not try and apply it to that pesky piano black trim that many B-pillars have? Piano black trim is notoriously easy to mark and can be difficult to polish to perfection, and being a relatively small area, it is quite straightforward to apply PPF. Offcuts are normally available online for very little outlay, and if it looks wrong, you can simply remove it and try again. Alternatively, you can buy kits for small areas such as mirrors or handles.

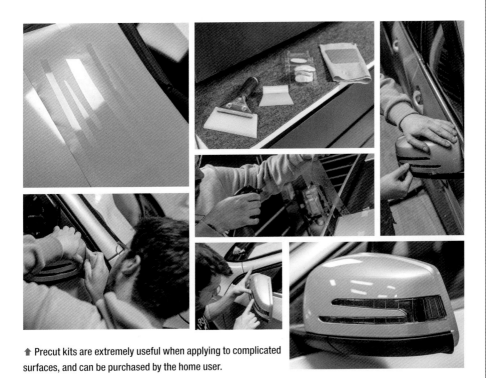

⬆ Precut kits are extremely useful when applying to complicated surfaces, and can be purchased by the home user.

Chapter 6

INTERIOR CLEANING & DETAILING

Machine polishing might be the glamorous side of detailing, but it's the interior that often makes the difference between victory and second place at a concours.

You might imagine that compared to the intricacies of paint correction, interior detailing will be straightforward and barely worth touching on. However, as any seasoned valeter will attest, making an interior perfect is just as skilled a job as throwing a machine polisher over a car.

To break it down into manageable stages, we will look at each material type in turn, and how to clean and protect it. We will also investigate how to remove specific stains and forms of contamination, as well as odour removal and using specialised equipment that many won't even know exist.

Before we begin actively cleaning a vehicle, it is always wise to remove any loose items – this includes rubbish, coins, spiders, fuel receipts and all the other debris that seem to accumulate in a car.

⬇ Always remove as much as you can before starting, like dog guards, and turn interior lights off.

If you have dog guards, luggage covers or child seats in the car, it would make sense to take them out too. The same goes for stick-on window blinds and phone chargers – basically anything that will get in your way or clog up your crevice tool. If you have an older vehicle where the interior lights don't automatically turn off after a couple of minutes, and you can't manually turn them off, consider removing the bulbs to avoid a flat battery after your day of hard graft, or pop it onto a trickle charger whilst you work. Disconnecting the battery is an option but it is useful to be able to move electric seats and power the windows up and down - plus you might loose all your radio presets.

CARPET CLEANING

With your newly cleared car, the first step is to vacuum out as much loose debris as possible. Remove any floor mats first, then start with the seat bases (lower cushion, not rails) so you don't force dirt into your leather during future manoeuvres, then work on the carpets from the outside in, again to avoid transfer from dirty areas to clean ones. Don't stretch from one side to the other – use all the doors to access each area – and be careful with the vacuum hose rubbing on painted surfaces.

With stubborn dirt, consider using a stiff polymer brush in unison with your crevice tool to agitate the dust and dirt out of the carpet fibres. If you have a dog hair issue, consider getting a rubber pet-hair brush to help comb them out, though a rubber Marigold-style glove can also be effective. As you move on to the centre console, switch to a softer brush to agitate the dust so you don't mark the plastic.

⬇ A wet vacuum can make carpet cleaning much quicker, and faster to dry.

⬇ Clean your floor mats outside of the vehicle.

Floor mats

The floor mats are designed to protect the carpet by taking the brunt of the wear and dirt. It is best to clean them away from the vehicle, ideally on a clean surface like your garage floor. Simply vacuuming them may be enough, so try using a stiff polymer brush as with the rest of the carpet. However, you may want to go slightly further and consider washing them more thoroughly. The easiest option is to spray on a suitably diluted APC or upholstery cleaner, scrub with a handheld brush, and then extract with a wet vac. You may need to repeat the process a couple of times, and then leave them in the sunshine or on a radiator to dry fully while getting on with the rest of the car.

You can spray rubber mats with an APC, agitate with a brush and then use a pressure washer to rinse. If you can hang the mats on a wall or fence, it will make the job easier, allowing you to rinse from top to bottom, prior to drying them as much as possible.

Top Tip

If you are leaving your mats near a heat source such as a radiator, ensure they do not get too hot or the rubber and plastic elements may melt. If your mats are particularly plush or delicate, such as real wool mats, consider placing next to a dehumidifier overnight rather than using heat, as it is a much gentler way to dry them.

For both floor mats and carpets, using steam can be an easy and efficient way to clean, particularly if they are heavily soiled or you're trying to remove a bad odour. With the carpet, try not to saturate it, as the sound deadening below can hold water and it can be very hard to extract it with a wet vac. There are lots of relatively cheap domestic steam cleaners on the market, with the main difference between entry-level and more expensive machines being the intensity and duration of the steam produced. As with the vacuum, be careful not to let the hose abrade the sills of the car when working, and remember that steam tends to be on the warm side of hot – it is very easy to burn yourself when contorted in a footwell!

Spot repairs

If you have specific stains in a mat or carpet that you want to remove, you will need to carry out a spot repair. First, identify what the stain is, as that will give you a steer as to what sort of chemical can be used.

Generally speaking, you have four genres of cleaning chemical: detergent, solvent, acid and alkali. By using the correct genre of cleaning chemical – and starting with a mild option is the safest route – gradually increase the strength and concentration of the products used until either the mark is removed or it is deemed too likely to damage the material further. You can also use heat in the form of steam, or, in some cases, extreme cold, such as freezing chewing gum off a surface. In an ideal situation, you want to keep physical abrasion to a minimum as this is what will most likely cause damage to the affected area. Use the table overleaf to help establish the chemical group or system on a certain stain.

⬆ Before tackling an interior it is worth stocking up on appropriate interior products.

Stain	Carpet	Hard plastic	Soft plastic	Fabric	Leather*	Alcantara**
Mud, dust, general dirt	Water or Diluted APC	Water or Diluted APC	Water or Diluted APC	Upholstery cleaner	Damp cloth	Lukewarm water
Organic (coffee, vomit, blood)	Enzyme-based cleaner	Enzyme-based cleaner	Enzyme-based cleaner	Enzyme-based cleaner	Water-based leather cleaner	Cold water, lemon juice
Oil, grease, lipstick, etc	Citrus or mild solvent	Citrus cleaner	Citrus cleaner	Warm water and APC	Solvent-based leather cleaner	Ethyl alcohol
Ink / dye	IPA-based cleaner and diluted APC	IPA-based cleaner	IPA-based cleaner	IPA-based cleaner	Solvent-based leather cleaner	Ethyl alcohol
Water-based paint	Diluted APC	Diluted APC	Diluted APC	Upholstery cleaner and APC	Water-based leather cleaner	Lukewarm water
Water / tide marks	Diluted vinegar	Diluted vinegar	Diluted vinegar	Diluted vinegar	Lukewarm water	Lemon juice

* Analine leather would require specialist cleaners. See p95 for more information on leather types.

** Alcantara-specific cleaners are recommended by the manufacturer in all instances, but if not available, suggestions in the table are a good backup.

FABRIC CLEANING

Fabric seat cleaning works on a similar principle to carpets, but you need to be more careful to ensure you don't rip out any threads or make any existing damage worse. The first step is vacuuming, paying particular attention to the seams and troughs where grot gathers.

For specific stain removal, follow the steps suggested for carpet cleaning using information in the table opposite. However, for a general 'freshen up' you can use a fabric cleaner or suitably diluted APC to make quite a difference with relative ease. Wet extraction can work very well on fabric seats, but be sure not to saturate them as many contain heating elements and occupancy sensors, and be aware that they may need a night in the company of a dehumidifier to dry fully.

Top Tip

When vacuuming seats, hold the bolsters apart to get better access with a crevice tool, and remember to manipulate the adjustable elements of the seat – tip the back backwards to get at the base of the seat, extend the thigh support (if equipped) to get into the crevice.

ODOUR REMOVAL

Removing a bad smell from a car can be an arduous process. In some cases it is easier simply to replace mats and carpets, such as if milk has been spilt and left in a warm vehicle for a week or two. The key is to remove the source of the smell using the techniques described above, not to just try and mask it with air fresheners.

Once you have dealt with the origin of the smell, you might want to consider using an anti-bacterial treatment to ensure it doesn't return. These range from little jars of chlorine-based gas that you leave in a vehicle overnight with the windows shut, to bigger machines like the Autosmart Aromatek, which is designed to kill bacteria and leave a pleasant smell in their place.

There are various fogging machines on the market, but be careful to ensure they aren't just masking a smell with overpowering perfume.

Top Tip

The cabin air filter should be changed on a regular basis as part of vehicle servicing, but they are often neglected. If you have a smell with no identifiable source or you have just deep cleaned a bad smell out of a vehicle, change the cabin filter at the same time. They are usually straightforward to swap out and not that expensive to buy.

HEADLINING

Headliners can be the bane of a detailer's life, particularly on older vehicles. Generally speaking, headliners on modern vehicles are hard-backed polyurethane foam with a fabric bonded over the top. Older vehicles use just fabric stretched between plywood or metal ribs. Over time, the adhesive used can degrade and the fabric detaches from the backing board, while on older types the fabric can stretch, leading to sagging. Improper cleaning techniques can accelerate both issues.

⬇ You can gently brush Alcantara in a single direction to make it look better.

Some higher end vehicles have Alcantara headlining – it has the appearance of suede but is in fact a synthetic material – which can be susceptible to 'bobbling'. If your car is so equipped, we would suggest extra caution, and avoid using anything but the softest brushes and mildest cleaners.

Regardless of the type of headlining, the most important thing is not to saturate the material – with cleaning chemicals or even just water. For lightly soiled linings, a mild APC sprayed onto a sponge, and then lightly dabbed onto the headliner will suffice. Follow this with gentle agitation with a soft or medium-soft brush to loosen

the dirt. This can then be wiped off with a microfibre – remember to turn the microfibre regularly to ensure you are removing the dirt, not simply relocating it.

For cars with heavy marking, such as brown tobacco stains, it may be possible to use a foam cleaner applied to a microfibre, which can then be gently 'massaged' into the surface. Do not be tempted to use stronger solvents or more concentrated cleaning chemicals – you're much better off repeating a process using gentler options than trying to fix it in a single aggressive hit.

On rare occasions steam can help with headlining, but the risk of melting the adhesive is high, as is the risk of oversaturating the material, so we would only suggest it as a last resort on a headliner that otherwise would be replaced.

Top Tip

As with many things in the world of detailing, it is important to know when to stop, when the risk of damage outweighs the chance of improvement. New headlining can be expensive and is always a tiresome job to fit.

⬇ This 20 year old Subaru headlining responded well to steam, but not all can survive it.

LEATHER CLEANING

More cars are equipped with leather or leather-effect upholstery than with fabric seats nowadays. In order to know how to treat leather, the first step is to understand what it is and the different types commonly found in cars.

The rest of this leather care and repair section will be based on pigmented leather or vinyl, as these are most commonly found in cars, and as their top surface is effectively the same, are treated in much the same manner.

If you have grubby seats the first product to try is water – as the polyurethane surface of leather is essentially a waterproof plastic, you can often remove dirt with a damp microfibre.

➡ People are often amazed at the difference when leather is cleaned properly.

Material type	Background
Vinyl	Often used on 'leather-effect' interiors, as well as on the sides and backs of seats that have 'real leather' fronts
Aniline leather (aka full grain)	The most expensive leather, very rarely used in cars – mostly for designer handbags and luxury goods. Sometimes used on high-end retrimmed cars. Semi-aniline is marginally more common
Pigmented leather	The most widely used form of 'real' leather. Often made from cow, horse or pig hide – vegan compliant alternatives are also becoming more common
Bicast leather (aka split leather)	The cheapest form of leather, often used for cheap goods that claim to be 'genuine leather'. Sometimes known as PU leather due to high polyurethane content
Nubuck leather	Often presented as a high-end leather; used primarily in footwear as it is tough and breathable, while still being waterproof
Napa leather	'Napa' refers to a process that leather is put through, invented in the Napa Valley of California
Suede	Not used in cars, though people often mistake Alcantara for suede
Alcantara	Fully synthetic material invented in Japan, and currently licensed by an Italian company. Cheap to make but has a 'high-end' image

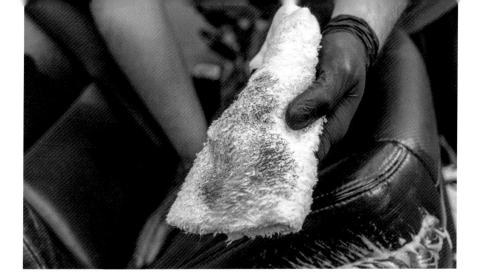

Composition	How to identify
Fully synthetic material, sometimes fabric-backed; many different types and qualities	Will feel cold to the touch and will stretch if you push your finger over it
Aniline is essentially uncoated leather, taken from the best bits of hide – usually higher up towards the surface of the animal; colour comes from a dying process, rather than being painted	It feels very soft and luxurious, but absorbs water, leading to staining, as there is no plastic top layer. The colour is present throughout the thickness of the material
Taken from middle regions of the hide, this leather is painted with colour and then coated with a polyurethane top layer. The texture is created artificially	Feels soft to the touch but if pressed with a finger, it won't stretch. Also absorbs heat so will feel 'room temperature' rather than cold like vinyl
Bicast is the chicken nugget of leather – low quality parts of the hide and offcuts are mulched together and mixed with various polymers. It is then 'cast' into a material and the leather texture is added with heat presses	As a reconstituted product, bicast is much more susceptible to splitting and cracking – usually looks more like plastic with an artificial gloss. When burned it smells toxic like plastic
Created from the lower regions of the hide, above where suede is taken but below where pigmented leather is taken. Sanded down to look smoother	Very rarely in cars; usually harder and stiffer than topcoat, lacks the 'luxury' feel
The napa 'process' happens during the tanning stage so can be aniline or pigmented leather	The same as pigmented leather, though softer to the touch and often looks smoother and less-textured
Taken from the inner part of the hide, dyed through the thickness of the material	Highly unlikely you will find it in a car, unless someone has left their blue shoes in the boot
Constructed of a polyester and polyurethane blend, with the colour added during the mixing process rather than painted on top	If it looks like suede and it is factory fitted to a car, it will be Alcantara. As a licensed product it may even have a small label somewhere declaring it to be 'official' Alcantara

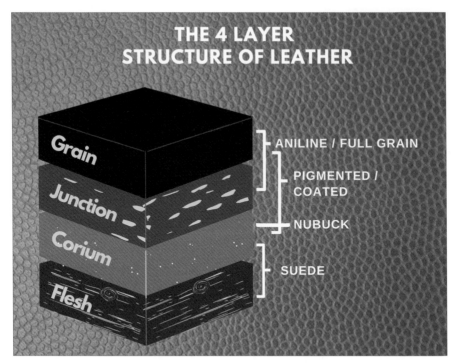

THE 4 LAYER STRUCTURE OF LEATHER

Grain — ANILINE / FULL GRAIN

Junction — PIGMENTED / COATED

— NUBUCK

Corium

Flesh — SUEDE

Should a damp cloth fail to remove everything, the next step is a mild, water-based leather cleaner. These often contain isopropyl alcohol and other detergents, and can remove most everyday marks from hide. Though we would always recommend following the manufacturer's instructions, it is often best to spray the cleaner onto a microfibre, then wipe on the surface and remove with a second clean microfibre. Spraying directly onto the surface can result in using more product and overspraying onto other surfaces in the car.

You can spray a cleaning solution directly onto the leather and then use a brush to agitate the dirt, before wiping off with a clean microfibre. There are various brushes advertised as safe for leather, but the best option, in our experience, is something called a Tampico brush. This is made from hollow fibres of the cactus plant, and though it feels quite stiff, when it gets moist it becomes softer and works nicely at removing dirt without degrading the surface. Whichever brush you use, don't work it too hard as you can wear away the protective coating.

For spot stain removal, there are stronger, solvent-based cleaners that will be more effective, but should be used with care. As leather is essentially a painted surface, there is always a risk of removing some of the colour.

Top Tip

Clean leather usually has a matte finish – the shine you get on leather is normally the dirt and grease that accumulates on it over the years.

This is particularly true on older, worn seats, as there will be less of the protective lacquer remaining.

Top Tip

Leather repair

Many people presume that a rip, tear, scuff or even burn cannot be repaired without retrimming all or part of the seat. In fact, it is possible to repair most minor damage in leather at home; there are plenty of repair kits available from companies like Furniture Clinic and Colourlock.

The process involves cleaning the leather with solvent cleaners then sanding back the area to be repaired, thus removing the lacquer layer and some of the colour coat.

⬇ Leather repair is quickly becoming popular among professional detailers.

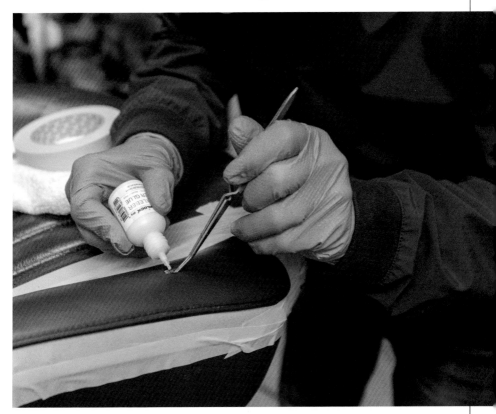

In some cases, a filler will need to be used to build the surface of the leather back up. Leather fillers tend to be flexible, so when cured they can bend with the surface. To replicate the texture of the rest of the seat, which will have been removed or distorted by the repair process, detailers take a sample imprint mould from another part of the seat and press it into the repair area before the top layer of filler has cured.

Many leather companies will mix the paint for your seats, either from a colour code or from a sample swatch (like a headrest). Alternatively, you can mix the colour yourself using a recipe based on your colour code, which you then tweak by eye to account for variations in factory colours and the fade that might have affected the rest of the interior over time. This is quite a skilled process, and while there are apps and colour measuring tools available, it ultimately relies on human judgement – if you are colour-blind, it is perhaps wise to leave it to the professionals.

Once the colour coat has been applied, often in multiple thin layers, you then spray a clear polyurethane top coat over the top, replicating a factory finish. Some companies produce additional protection products designed to be applied over the lacquer, which add slickness, further improving the protection.

Leather protection

You may well have heard of the term 'leather feed' and no doubt have seen a few products that claim to condition the leather like skin moisturisers. However, as discussed, leather is in fact coated with an layer of polyurethane, which is synthetic and bears little resemblance to organic skin - this would need to break down before conditioners reached actual leather. Nevertheless, there is good reason to apply leather protection products to the topcoat and indeed the vinyl parts of your car. These create a sacrificial layer that helps stop dirt and grease from penetrating the top layers of your hide. They also often contain UV filters to help resist the fading effect that eventually occurs from sunlight. Finally, they create lower friction, making it harder for dirt to adhere to the surface.

It is best to follow the manufacturer's instructions when it comes to application, but there are two important things to get right with almost every single product. The first is preparation – there is little point in applying these products to dirty seats; in fact, it may have a detrimental effect. If you have set aside an hour for some leather love, spend most of that time cleaning, rather than loading on layers of protector. Secondly, less is generally more, so apply multiple thin layers regularly over time, rather than a solitary thick one once. The products are all designed to leave a very thin layer of protection, so by shovelling it on you are wasting product and making it harder for a strong layer to cure properly.

← Leather can be spray painted in much the same way as a car body is, base coat followed by lacquer.

HARD SURFACE CLEANING AND PROTECTION

When detailers refer to hard surfaces on a car interior they are talking about a multitude of different materials, from the clear plastic that sits in front of the speedometer to the wood-effect trim in the central binnacle.

The first step to cleaning the hard surfaces is to remove as much dirt as you can without making direct contact with the surface, just as the pre-wash stage works on the exterior. Use your vacuum with a crevice tool, or better still a soft brush attachment, and go over all the areas you can access. This will remove a lot of the larger particles of dust, hair and dirt without potentially marking the surface with abrasion.

Top Tip

For added safety, wrap a couple of layers of electrical insulation tape around the tip of your crevice tool to make it softer. Also, be careful with the vacuum hose over door sills and other areas where it might rub during use.

You will find a good selection of specialist tools and accessories for vacuuming car interiors online, including brushes and miniature crevice tools.

⬇ Using a brush to agitate dust makes vacuuming more effective.

The latter may well have extra holes on them, which should not be blocked, as most vacuum cleaners will be unduly stressed by being forced to suck through such a small aperture. When vacuuming with a crevice tool, consider using a soft detailing brush to gently agitate surface dust and encourage it to lift off into the vacuum.

Once you have removed as much loose detritus as possible, work on the more stubborn muck. For light soiling, you can just wet a microfibre with clean water, and wipe over a surface, though many will find a diluted APC or dedicated interior cleaning detergent quicker and more effective. To avoid spraying water or cleaning products all over the interior, apply them directly to a microfibre outside of the car, and remember to turn the microfibre regularly, folding the dirty parts inside to reveal the clean parts.

Top Tip

Have a bucket of clean water by the car so you can rinse out your microfibres and brushes as you go

For heavily soiled areas, particularly those with a profound texture, you might need to spray your cleaning product directly onto the surface. In which case, try to shield any surrounding areas such as textile, leather or glass from the spray.

Once you have sprayed the product on, use a brush to ensure it gets right into the texture of the plastic – if it is a really filthy panel, consider rinsing the brush out occasionally too. Once complete, try to dry the area quickly so as to not let the cleaning solution dry on the surface.

When a product is left to dry, the water content evaporates off first, which potentially increases the concentration of the active ingredients beyond a safe level. At best, this can leave tide marks that will need removing; at worst, it can damage more delicate surfaces.

Should you come across certain stains, try and identify what the mark is before choosing the type of cleaning product to use. With most plastic trim you need to avoid solvents, as these can react with the plastic and make them go milky or, worse still, start to remove the 'soft-touch' rubberised coatings. For non-organic marks, steam can be an effective tool, but always test on an inconspicuous area first, as some materials are sensitive to heat and can be damaged with steam. For organic marks, using a slightly stronger detergent cleaner or possibly an alcohol-based alternative would be the sensible course of action, but avoid heat.

For many people, clean trim with a natural look is all they want to achieve with an interior detail. However, there are numerous dressings and protection products on the market, which can be applied after an area has been cleaned. Some cleaning products also claim to add an element of protection too, ranging from cheap silicone-based products that leave a glossy sheen – ideal for creating reflections on the inside of the windscreen and attracting dust – to more advanced water-based alternatives that leave a matte finish and can sometimes have anti-static properties.

Many of these areas are cleaned in the same way, but there are certain surfaces and materials where extra caution or a different strategy is needed.

TFT screens	It wasn't long ago when a little dot-matrix digital clock was considered cutting edge for cars, but now huge thin-film-transistor (TFT) screens are replacing conventional audio and ventilation controls, as well as smaller screens replacing analogue speedometers and fuel gauges. Many of these have delicate coatings on to reduce glare and reflections, which can be easily damaged by alcohol cleaners and even some detergents. Mobile phone screens might use similar technology, but they have much tougher surfaces that can resist both chemical and physical abuse. TFT screens are also vulnerable to abrasion, so do not use paper towels, which are actually quite abrasive; a soft microfibre or microsuede is far more suitable.

Use an alcohol and ammonia-free cleaning solution designed for screens, ideally with a medium-pile microfibre cloth. Be careful not to simply move the dirt into the edges and corners of the screen; instead wipe inwards so you can lift it away with the microfibre, and remember to use very little pressure when wiping – better to wipe lightly three times than wiping once forcefully and then having to explain why half of the pixels don't work.

Top Tip

It sounds obvious, but make sure the screen is switched off when you are wiping it! With touchscreens you might end up changing all sorts of settings, and with all screens, the heat output when turned on will make your cleaning solution evaporate more quickly. You are also more likely to damage the screen if you put too much pressure on it while powered up.

Primary control surfaces	This refers to things like the brake pedal, gear knob and steering wheel. Do not apply any protection products to these areas – greasy silicone on a brake pedal is a recipe for disaster. If you are treating the leather on a steering wheel or handbrake, make sure it has dried completely before driving the car. To clean pedals, use a correctly diluted APC and a medium-stiff brush to agitate the mud out of the tread panel. Then dry methodically with a microfibre.

Piano black trim	Gloss black painted plastic trim has been the vogue for nearly a decade, and while it can look very smart, the surface is notoriously easy to mark, just like the piano black trim that often adorns B- and C-pillars on the outside of a car. Most damage to these components happens during daily use of the car – putting the house keys in the cup holder, or even the zip from a big jacket can do a lot of harm. While these areas can be machine polished back in many cases, it makes sense to try and avoid damaging them further during cleaning. There's no particular strategy or trick to be employed here – vacuuming followed by gentle wiping with a damp microfibre is the best option – but just take extra care and time over these areas.
Wood trim	Most wood-effect trim in cars is hydro-dipped plastic with a lacquer sprayed on top. Even if it is real wood, the chances are that a lacquer has been applied on top to add a gloss and seal the wood. However, in the olden days they did use a big, porous plank of wood for dashboards, and therefore, saturating it with APC and trying to wipe it off with a microfibre will be a disappointing experience. Without wanting to delve too deeply into the realms of carpentry, the first thing you need to establish is whether the wood is natural, stained or varnished, and what condition the said finish is in. If there is flaking varnish evident, the best bet would be to leave it well alone and find a craftsman or delicate-fingered lumberjack to restore it. If natural or stained and in good condition, old-fashioned wood wax would be the best bet – Swissvax actually make a product designed specifically for wood dashboards.
Recessed switches	Many electric window switches have recessed cavities into which one inserts a finger to operate. These cavities are often too small for a crevice tool or detailing brush to penetrate, so a new strategy is called for. Detailers are often teased for using cotton buds on switch gear and ventilation grilles, but a cotton bud moistened with APC can be a lifesaver – just don't talk about it at social gatherings. Other options include micro sponges made by the likes of Hygan, which are designed specifically for this somewhat niche application. You can also use wooden cocktail sticks to get grot out of the gaps between switches – it really boils down to how much time and patience you possess.
Touch-sensitive switches	The latest cars have ditched buttons and knobs in favour of touch-sensitive panels and laptop-style touch pads, often with haptic feedback functions. In principle these are easy to clean and reduce the number of crevices that dirt can get wedged in. However, they will doubtless be more sensitive than old-fashioned switchgear, so be careful not to over-saturate them or abrade the surface.
Temperature sensors	If you look very carefully at the interior of your car, you may notice a little grille, usually less than 8mm square, that looks almost like a tweeter. This might be a tweeter, the small speakers designed to play high-frequency sound; but it may be the internal temperature sensor for your climate control – a very delicate little thermocouple. If you come across it, do not spray anything anywhere near to it, and certainly don't poke dirt or your cocktail stick into it. It has happened before, and the results have been… chilling.

⬆ Remember - if equipped - to disconnect batteries and airbags carefully before removing seats.

Airbag connections	If you are having a particularly in-depth session, you may well come across yellow plugs, normally under the seats and around the seat belt bases. These connect your airbags and your seat belt pre-tensioners to the car's computer. Airbags are inflated by explosive charges and pre-tensioners also use nitrocellulose, and while cars have various safety systems in place to stop accidental discharge, one can never be too careful. Try to avoid touching them, and if you are disconnecting them to remove the seat, disconnect the car battery half an hour before tinkering. For those who didn't heed the instructions above, the white dust that now coats the interior of your car is a combination of talcum powder, sodium hydroxide and sometimes potassium chloride. It's quite toxic, so don a respirator before continuing your interior detail.
Seat belts	Seat belts are often forgotten about in the cleaning process, even though they sit in the line of fire when it comes to guzzling that motorway coffee or croissant while on the move, or perhaps the odd surprise sneeze. The important things to know when cleaning seat belts is to remember to pull them all the way out, and not to use any harsh chemicals on them. A spray of correctly diluted APC followed by a gentle rub with a medium-soft brush, and thorough dry with a microfibre is all that's required. Try and get them as dry as possible before releasing them back into their cubby hole. Anything containing ammonia, bleach, or a particularly extreme pH is not recommended.

Chapter 7

CLEANING AND DETAILING EVERYTHING ELSE

In the introduction, we discussed the definition and etymology of 'detailing' as a term, revealing that it means different things to different people in different countries, and that perhaps it is best described as an existential attitude towards car care. One could suggest it is these following finishing touches that make the difference between a really well prepared car, and a detailed car.

GLASS

The glass should be attended to last of all when detailing the interior of a vehicle because it is easy to accidentally spray cleaning products or leave the odd fingerprint when attending to other areas.

There are three genres of glass cleaner – the most popular is isopropyl alcohol (IPA) based, which is good at removing grease and fingerprints. Acid based – or more commonly vinegar-based – cleaners are also useful, particularly if battling mineral deposits and water marks. Finally, there are the emulsions, which are often marketed as polishes due to a very slight abrasive content – these work well on heavily soiled screens, particularly at removing cooked-on bird lime and bug carcasses.

⬇ A few simple tips can make glass cleaning much easier.

It is always wise to start on the outside of the glass, which should have already received a wash as part of the main contact wash. We would suggest using either an IPA-based cleaner, or a vinegar-based alternative, sprayed onto a microfibre cloth and then wiped in straight horizontal lines. Use a clean cloth to remove any residue, again in straight horizontal lines.

Top Tip

To make sure you get the top of the glass, drop the window down an inch so you can clean the top edge, and raise it up again to get the bottom section.

If the glass is still not looking as good as you would like, you can use an emulsion polish, or alternatively you can always use a clay bar in much the same way you would on paint. Glass is much harder than paint and therefore harder to scratch, but it is still worth using a lubricant – either a clay lube or 'quick detailer' – most glass cleaners won't lubricate particularly well and any solvent-based glass cleaners may adversely affect the clay. You will need to clean your windows again after claying to remove the residue, particularly if using some quick detailer. Also consider using a clay cloth as opposed to a clay bar – they are just as effective and harder to drop.

Once the outside has been cleaned, you will need to do the inside. IPA-based glass cleaner is particularly effective on the inside of glass as most of the typical contamination is easily broken down by the alcohol. You shouldn't need to clay the inside of your glass. The methodology is the same, apply glass cleaner to a

microfibre, and wipe in straight lines, but this time wipe in vertical lines. As before, take a second clean microfibre and buff off in vertical straight lines.

Now stand back and look at your glass from lots of different angles – can you see any smears? If you can and they are going up and down the glass, you need to buff the inside off again. If they are left to right, you need to buff the outside off. Don't forget to clean the wing mirrors at this point too – depending on how long you have spent on the rest of the car, they may even have stopped dripping from the main wash by now – as well as rear-view and vanity mirrors.

Though there is nothing quite like driving a car with perfectly clear glass, you can go a step further and add a hydrophobic glass sealant. There are, broadly speaking, two types of glass sealant: silane-based, and siloxane-based. Siloxane-based products are much easier to apply but don't bond as strongly and thus don't last as long as their silane-based alternatives.

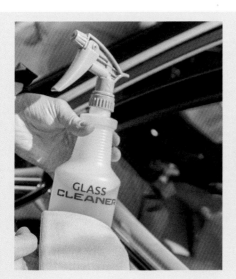

1 Take a suitable glass cleaner and a lint-free, short-pile microfibre.

2 Apply the glass cleaner directly to the microfibre.

3 Clean the top of the dropped window, including the edge, first of all.

4 You will be amazed how dirty the top edge is.

5 Spray cleaner onto the outside and wipe horizontally.

6 Spray cleaner onto the microfibre and wipe vertically for the inside face, then check for streaks.

↑ There is a huge selection of hydrophobic glass sealants available on the market.

Both types of sealant will offer three key benefits compared to unprotected glass: greater resilience to freezing over on winter mornings; ease of cleaning off dirt in the future; and perhaps most impressively, the ability to make water fly off at speed without using the windscreen wipers.

Just like driving in a blizzard at night with your full beams on, there is something surreal when driving at 70mph on the motorway in the rain with the wipers off and water just sliding off the screen – it should be on the bucket list of any car care enthusiast!

The siloxane-based sealants are normally spray-and-wipe affairs, though some require a little curing time between application and removal.

All of them work best when the screen has been properly cleaned and decontaminated. The latest products are even available as screen wash concentrates so the water repellency is topped up every time you squirt; though a word of warning, these often need to be mixed in higher concentrations than

typical anti-freeze during winter, and they can smear more than other screen wash products.

The silane-based products are even more reliant on having a perfectly clean surface, and often benefit from extended curing periods for best effect. As ever, it is essential to read the instructions fully prior to even starting the process – not halfway through when you suddenly realise you need to drive the car through the rain to get to work in ten minutes.

← Soft99 make a self-priming glass sealant for ultimate ease.

TRIM

Exterior trim is a term that usually refers to the plastic strips that go along the sides of doors to protect them in car parks. They can be painted or left a 'natural' black colour, and some older cars have metal strips within them as an aesthetic addition. Those that are painted should be treated like the rest of the painted surfaces, though if polishing, remember they are plastic and retain heat more than metal, so need to be treated with extra care.

⬇ Trim dressing can help slow the fading process on rubber trim.

For 'natural' black plastic trims the biggest problem is fade, where they go a lighter grey colour over time thanks to UV-catalysed oxidation that breaks down the pigmentation within the polymer. This can happen to any unpainted plastics on a vehicle; in particularly sunny countries it even happens to interior plastics such as those on top of the dashboard, which eventually crack and disintegrate.

⬆ The range of ceramic trim sealants is plentiful.

There are four ways that people can rectify and restore the colour: trim dressings, trim sealants, trim restorers and the 'heat gun trick'. Trim dressings will instantly darken the finish; they are easy to apply; and the better ones can last as long as an organic wax thanks to complex silicones and UV filters. Trim sealants are similar to ceramic paint and silane-based glass sealants; while they are more involved to apply, they can last around a year, if not longer. Trim restorers, as the name suggests, are more about restoring the colour as opposed to protection, and they do this with miniscule carbon particles that bond to the carbon-based plastic trim. You can often apply a trim dressing or sealant over the top of restorers for ultimate longevity.

⬆ Solution Finish is among the best trim restorers.

The 'heat gun trick' is not one to be recommended. It probably won't be a huge surprise to hear that it involves running a heat gun along the trim, which essentially melts the top layer of plastic. While this does indeed darken the trim in the short term, it accelerates the drying out process that is partly to blame for the fading in the first place. It is very much a short-term fix favoured by certain unscrupulous second-hand car dealers rather than a legitimate detailing technique.

⬇ Some trim dressings work best when applied via a soft sponge.

⬇ Restoring faded trim can make a profound visual improvement.

Top Tip

As many trim dressing products contain silicone, do not apply them anywhere near where paint is being applied, and wherever you do apply them, apply the product to a microfibre and then to the trim. Do not spray them directly onto your car – even if the instructions tell you to.

⬅ Don't believe the old wives tale about peanut butter being good at restoring trim - the oils darken it but the finish is short-lived compared to proper dressings.

WHEELS

Watch any professional detailing video and you will see that detailers remove the wheels from a car pretty much straight after it has been washed. This is normally so they can be cleaned thoroughly and then have a protective coating applied. You don't have to remove wheels to clean and protect them, but it does make life easier, and you can do a more thorough job of it.

If you are keeping the wheels on the car but still wish to protect them, the first step is to ensure they are as clean as possible – instructions are in the wash section of this book. With the wheels in place, your best option is wheel wax, as it is easy to apply and, depending on the spoke design of your alloys, you can coat much of the inner barrel without too much difficulty. Wheel wax is similar to conventional wax for paintwork, but is generally designed to withstand higher temperatures at the cost of reduced gloss compared to the best show waxes. Depending on your driving style and mileage, you can expect a good wheel wax to last a month, maybe more. Being a relatively inert substance, you can usually use wheel wax safely on diamond-cut and even anodised finishes.

For those removing wheels to give you better access, you may wish to consider a ceramic-type sealant. These take more time and care to apply, and are much less tolerant of poorly cleaned surfaces, but do outlast wheel waxes several times over, sometimes enduring for two years. The details of application vary between products, but the general procedure is just

Top Tip

If you choose to remove your wheels in order to detail them, please be sensible about lifting your vehicle. Professional detailers use scissor lifts and carefully research where the safe jacking points are on a vehicle. Lifting your car with the supplied emergency jack on a steep gravel driveway in the rain is a recipe for disaster – cars can get damaged, as will their owners, so be safe.

like a ceramic coat-on paint, using a microsuede cloth wrapped around a foam block to apply in straight lines. This will need buffing before being left to dry for a few hours, sometimes even overnight.

➡ There are plenty of gadgets to help you, including wheel stands and lug nut organisers.

⬅ Wheel waxes can withstand higher temperatures than normal wax.

TYRES

Tyres can hold a remarkable amount of dirt, and not just in their treads. While the main contact wash may get them looking cleaner, to get them truly clean will take some extra elbow grease.

Though rubber is a natural product, tyres don't grow ready to roll on Pirelli trees, and only about 30–40% of a tyre is of organic origin – the remainder is made up of all sorts of chemicals from styrene-butadiene to sulphur. To shorten a potentially very long and detailed story, rubber is porous and as a consequence it can stubbornly retain contamination. You may find several rounds of cleaning are necessary to get back to black.

⬆ Dedicated tyre cleaners are becoming more popular, though APC works very nearly as well.

In terms of a cleaning regime, start with a shampoo and a scrubbing brush to remove the mud. Then you can move on to something with a little more bite – an all purpose cleaner (APC) can work well to get rid of the more ingrained dirt.

Strangely, vinegar, when diluted 1:10, can work wonders too – ideally the cheapest vinegar you can find in the supermarket – balsamic just won't do. Between steps, dry the tyre with a microfibre and keep repeating the step until the microfibre doesn't get marked from dirt being removed. There are some dedicated tyre cleaners out there, and while tests have shown them to be marginally more effective than APC, they're a 'nice to have' rather than an essential buy.

Once you have cleaned the tyre to perfection, or more likely decided that two hours of your weekend cleaning the parts of your car that will get dirty again within two minutes is not worth it, you can think about tyre dressings. There are water-based and silicone-based options; the former tend to leave a nice natural finish, the latter a shiny 'wet-look'. In both cases you can normally adjust the levels of gloss with your application method – if you want less gloss you can apply to a microfibre, wipe on to the tyre, and then wipe off with a clean microfibre. If you want the gloss turned up to 11, you can literally paint it on with a brush and either leave to dry naturally, or, if it starts to look a bit patchy, use a microfibre cloth to gently level out the finish. Some like to pour layer upon layer of dressing on, but beware of it flinging straight off the tyre and onto your nice clean bodywork when you drive off.

METAL POLISHING

Chrome used to be a major feature of cars back when everything was black and white, and most people of a certain age would spend a significant part of their Sunday fervently polishing their bumper overriders. Modern cars still have the odd shiny bit, but this is almost invariably a chrome-effect coating over plastic, not 'proper' chrome-plated steel. Even exhaust tail pipe trims that used to be stainless steel are now more likely to be plastic, with the actual exhaust pipe recessed well away from view.

⬇ Some higher-end cars have real metal trim, but with delicate anodised finishes. On older vehicles these may have been damaged irreparably by caustic wash products and discoloured or matted.

Whatever you do, do not use a metal polish on these faux metal surfaces – the chances are that you will damage the finish and reveal the plastic that lies beneath. Secondly, consider the type of metal you are polishing, as aluminium is much softer than stainless steel, so you will need to approach it differently.

Top Tip

When cleaning faux metal trim or anodised metal strips, be sure to avoid using strong chemicals. Extremes of pH can cause stains to be etched into the finish, which are often impossible to remove.

⬆ Stainless steel can polish up very nicely.

There is an abundance of metal polishes available, and many can be used by hand and machine. Metal polish works in two ways. Firstly, it contains solvents that chemically remove stains and the blooms of rust that grow around a pin-prick hole on chrome-plated steel. Secondly, they have physical abrasives suspended in a lubricating emulsion, designed to abrade off the top layer of oxidised metal. If you are polishing aluminium, such as the rims of deep-dish alloys, it may well be wise to source a polish that relies more on the solvent power than the abrasive cut to achieve a mirror finish. Equally your choice of medium is important, as wire wool, for example, will be much more effective at removing corrosion but a microfibre will create a finer finish.

Also consider if the metal surface you are trying to polish is designed to be shiny – galvanised steel, for example, cannot be brought up to a mirror finish without removing the zinc coating and the rust protection it brings. The most common example of metal damage is on anodised aluminium, which went through a popular phase from about 2000 to the mid-2010s. An owner would try to clean them with a caustic product, causing staining, and then attempt to polish off the milky marks with an abrasive, and in so doing, they would remove the thin anodised layer.

Many metal polishes claim a protective ability, though we would recommend a dedicated protection product for ultimate durability. Protecting bare metal is mostly about keeping oxygen away from the surface, so anything from a wax to specialised ceramic coating will work to some extent.

➡ There is a vast range of metal polishes on the market.

HEADLIGHT RESTORATION

Most modern cars are equipped with polycarbonate headlights which, despite many being coated at the factory, eventually become cloudy and in some cases turn slightly yellow. This is because of oxidation, catalysed by UV light from the sun. Some headlights will start to go cloudy much sooner than others, which is normally related to the quality of the factory coating, the specific formulation of the polycarbonate, and whether overly aggressive chemicals have been used to wash the car.

Oxidation usually occurs from the outer surface and gradually works into the thickness of the lens, so the sooner lights are restored and protected, the less the long-term damage will be. The restoration process removes the upper, oxidised layers of plastic, revealing the clear material underneath.

⬇ This Mitsubishi has oxidation on the top surface of the headlights.

Top Tip

While it is possible to restore headlights when they are on the vehicle, you will need to carefully mask the area around the lights to protect them from accidentally damaging surrounding paint and trim. Before masking up, have a look online to see how easy it is to remove the headlights from your particular vehicle – on many cars there are only two or three bolts holding the lights on and these can be removed in a matter of minutes. With the lights removed from the car, they will be much easier and safer to work on, and there is no risk of overspray if latterly applying a coat of lacquer to them. It still might be necessary to tape around the rubber seals on the lamp unit.

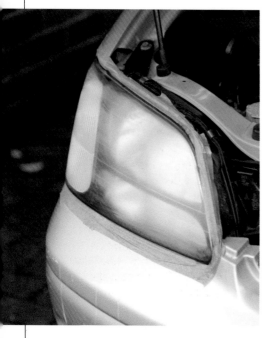

After wet sanding, a headlight will likely look worse than when you started.

The first step is wet sanding back, by hand or machine, and then polishing the surface with compound, much like you would polish paint. Some cars need more work than others, with extreme cases requiring P800 sandpaper to be used, though most only need finer P1000 or P2000 to remove the 'dead' layer. Once sanded, the lights will look even worse than when you started – quite often they will be completely opaque – but don't panic, simply go back over the surface with increasingly fine sandpaper, usually up to about P4000.

You can use ordinary compounds to polish up plastic headlights, though using a DA is safer than rotary for the inexperienced.

At this point you can switch to compounds, ideally used with a small DA polishing machine, and gradually work the surface back to an 'as new' transparency.

Many people make the mistake of considering the job finished at this point. However, if left unprotected, particularly as any remaining protection from the factory coating will also have been removed, the lights will go misty within weeks. Protection is key, and the main element you need to protect against is UV light, for which a polymer sealant is a good bet. There are various 'ceramic coating'-style products that are marketed specifically for headlights with claimed durability of over a year. However, the best option is to apply a layer of paint lacquer to simulate the protection applied at the factory.

Good-quality lacquer contains UV filters and can outlast any conventional polymer or ceramic protection product. A third option would be paint protection film (PPF), which offers even greater levels of physical protection on top of the UV shield.

The final word on headlights is one of caution. Depending on the car, some headlights are prone to condensation as a consequence of poor sealing. This leads to dirt ingress, which many attempt to solve by opening the unit to clean it on the inside. While the process can go to plan, it often doesn't, as people don't realise how delicate the silver reflective paint can be – a paper towel and water can strip it right off – so the general message is, don't touch the shiny bits if you can avoid them!

⬇ Ceramic coatings have been developed for headlamps as an alternative to lacquer.

CONVERTIBLE HOODS

In the early days of the motorcar, having a metal roof was considered a bit flash. Even a windscreen was optional. Conversely, nowadays a fabric roof is considered a sporting luxury for that wind-in-your-hair and flies-in-your-teeth experience. Originally, soft-tops were little more than impregnated cloth stretched over a metal frame that would offer a smidgen of protection in the event of a light shower. As material science improved, new materials were adopted, such as butyl rubber, rayon, latex and mohair. Modern equivalents are much more advanced

⬇ Convertible hoods can hold a remarkable amount of dirt and contamination.

multi-layer composites crafted over complex electric folding systems, with some having up to five different layers.

A typical soft top will be constructed in three layers: an upper woven fabric that offers physical protection; an elastomeric layer that is primarily there as a sound and water barrier; and then a second fabric layer that is more decorative than functional. Our focus when cleaning hoods is to get as much dirt and biological contamination out of the top layer, without pushing it into – and potentially damaging – the second layer. The third internal layer can be cleaned in a similar manner to a conventional headlining.

A typical cleaning procedure would be to spray on a fabric cleaner or appropriately diluted APC, then agitate it into the fibres of that outer layer with a medium detailing brush, brushing with the grain of the material. A soft brush probably won't get the cleaning solution far enough into the material, while a stiff brush risks damaging the weave. The roof should then be rinsed with either a hose pipe, or a pressure washer used at a distance on its lowest power setting. Do not use a jet washer on a high-pressure setting at close range or you will do more harm than good.

↥ Some protection products require convertibles to be completely dry.

Top Tip

You may see rotary or drill brush attachments being marketed as suitable for use on convertible roofs; while many have used these tools successfully, plenty have also come unstuck and caused damage. If you want to involve a machine in your cleaning process, use a medium-soft brush attachment on a DA machine, as these will stall if they get snagged or too much pressure is applied.

For hoods that have been neglected for a long time, you may see signs of green growth. This is caused by the fact that the upper layer retains water, making a damp environment. Add to this the fact that it is normally black or a dark colour, which absorbs heat, and you can understand that certain biological nasties do rather well – fungus, moss and algae all prosper in poorly maintained convertibles. To combat this, follow the cleaning procedure above, repeating as required until all signs of life have been removed.

Following the clean, apply a biocide product, be that an anti-bacterial or a fungicide, and work it into the fabric with a brush. This will kill any remaining organic matter and dissuade any newly introduced organisms from growing for a while.

Once clean, you have two further steps you may wish to follow to get your hood looking good. The first is to restore, or even change, the colour. The combination of UV light in the presence of oxygen, and overly harsh cleaning chemicals can break down the pigment in roof dyes and produce a faded finish. Often a good clean will restore the colour to a satisfactory level, but if you want more, various companies such as Renovo and Furniture Clinic produce dyes specifically for fabric roofs. Some can be used on moist surfaces, but some only work well if the fabric is bone dry, so read the instructions carefully, and be prepared to do multiple layers to get a good, consistent finish.

Once you have cleaned your roof, the next step is to protect it. There is a range of protection products out there, but whichever you chose, make sure it offers both a barrier to organic invasion and some form of UV protection. As with the colouring products, there are protection products that rely on the hood being completely dry and ones that aren't so demanding. Equally, multiple layers can add to the protection, but check with the manufacturer as to whether this is the case on your chosen product.

Top Tip

When drying your roof, use a lint-free, short-pile microfibre. There are few things more annoying in life than picking out little threads from a linting towel on a dark convertible roof prior to applying a protection product. If you read this after that particular horse has bolted, use a lint roller to accelerate the process, or a brush and hoover to pick up any remaining fluff and fibres

← Fabric dyes can be ordered in pretty much any colour, but common colours are available off the shelf from the likes of Renovo and Furniture Clinic.

↓ Applying dye to produce a consistent finish takes practice and patience in equal measure.

ENGINE BAY

Many loathe cleaning the engine bay, while others question the point of it when it is rarely seen (unless your car happens to be particularly unreliable and you're keen to impress your chosen breakdown recovery patrol person). However, for those of us who do like a clean motor, there are some important points to consider when cleaning and detailing it. A quick word of warning, for those with older cars particularly: one needs to be careful when introducing water and steam into the engine compartment, as electrics are

somewhat vulnerable and you can end up causing damage.

You may need to be mechanically minded to know what different components are under the bonnet, and which ones need particular care taken around them. If some of the technical terms used here are alien, do take the time to look them up and work out where they are on your vehicle.

Also, importantly, don't work on a hot engine – however careful you are you will burn yourself, usually at the wrist when reaching past a hot pipe to access some other part with a microfibre.

⬇ Classic engine bays have more exposed metalwork than modern ones.

↟ Some people take engine bay cleaning to more extreme levels than others.

There are four main materials that are commonly found in a typical engine bay: plastic, rubber, painted metal and bare metal. The more modern the vehicle, the more plastic there will be, which is good news when it comes to cleaning.

To clean the plastic components, a diluted APC sprayed directly onto the component, followed by agitation with a medium brush and a wipe off with a microfibre, is normally all that is needed. If the part is particularly dirty, consider using steam or a degreaser – though test the latter on an inconspicuous area first as stronger products can discolour some plastics.

For rubber components, mostly pipes, apply APC to a microfibre and wipe them down, taking a second microfibre to dry them off. Avoid using steam or more aggressive chemicals to prevent damaging important parts. Whereas with some plastic cladding parts, it is often easier to remove them and clean them away from the car, we would strongly recommend not removing any pipes for cleaning unless you are mechanically gifted and very determined to win your next show and shine competition.

Painted metal is normally body coloured and most common on the slam panel and around the suspension strut towers. Most modern cars have sound-deadening material covering much of the inside of the bonnet, but you can often clean around this too and it makes a real difference to the overall under-bonnet ambiance if you do. As before, judicious use of APC, agitated with a brush and wiped down with a microfibre is the best bet.

One thing to note: many cars don't have clear coat applied to painted surfaces under the bonnet, so do not be tempted to use a solvent degreaser without checking first, otherwise the paint will be missing from the car, and appear all over your microfibre.

Bare metal is more common in older vehicles; you will find lots of exposed metal at junctions on high-pressure pipes, and the distribution block that covers the ABS pump is often a billet block of aluminium. Once you have gone through the now familiar process using APC, being careful not to use caustic products, steam is the next step. Obviously be careful around these fittings, and if ever in doubt, leave it alone.

Look on the internet and you will often see people using pressure washers and high-pressure steam cleaners on engine bays. For those with modern cars, it is perfectly feasible to use a pre-wash style product, including snow foam, on an engine bay, which is then jetted off after a suitable dwell time. However, use a low pressure setting on the jet wash, and keep a good metre or so away from the engine – they are designed to withstand water from driving through a puddle, not 200 bar fired directly at it.

A steam cleaner is perhaps the most useful tool when it comes to engine bays, particularly when paired with a good degreaser for the really grimy areas. However, while electrical components are designed to cope with water in liquid form, steam is a whole different ball game and can quite often pressure through *water*proof seals. As a consequence,

while a hose can be used carefully in certain circumstances to rinse an engine bay, steam should only be used on specific areas and not as a general 'wash down' method. If a pipe does comes adrift and leaks fluid, clean it up as quickly as possible - power steering fluid, for example, is aggressive stuff.

Top Tip

If you are planning on a comprehensive clean, particularly if using a pressure washer, consider protecting key parts with clear plastic bags taped and cable tied around them. This can include alternators, fuse boxes, stand-alone coils, MAF sensors and ECUs. Remember to remove the bags after the wash and before driving the car.

➡ You can make a big improvement with just APC and a brush.

PAINT CHIP REPAIR

Paint chips are almost unavoidable unless you transport your car on a covered trailer, apply PPF or a 'bonnet bra', or even plaster the front of your car with 'scene tape' – the latter we strongly recommend against. When it comes to minor paint damage such as stone chips, road rash or minor scuffs, you have various options open to you. At one extreme you can take the vehicle to a paint shop to have the panel resprayed and blended into the rest of the bodywork, or you can use a mobile Small to Medium Area Repair Technique (SMART) service. At the other extreme, you can just not look at it and pretend it isn't there – which is free, until you come to sell the car and have to reduce the price when the buyer spots them and has a

⬇ Paint chip repair kits are available over the counter, or custom made to a paint code.

moan. Thankfully, there is another option – you can repair them to a pretty high standard yourself in many cases.

You can buy all manner of stone chip repair kits, which range from a simple 'pen' style up to more comprehensive packages that include brushes, paints, lacquers and sealants. Whichever of these you choose, you need to remember that the paints are mixed to a recipe provided by car manufacturers. This doesn't take into account the exact hue of your particular car as it left the factory, and it can't take into account any fade or degradation that might have happened since your car was painted. The only way to get an exact match is to visit a body shop equipped with a colour scanner and paint mixing machine, and even then, getting the right metallic fleck or pearlescent tint can be a challenge.

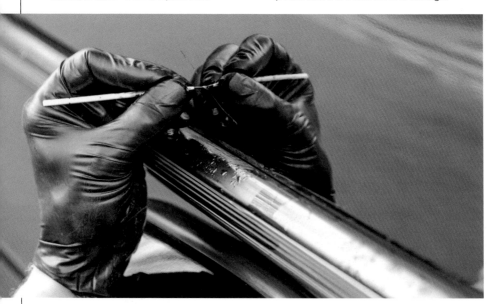

Some colours are harder to match than others by their nature, and some colours fade quicker than others too, while the way in which the paint is applied can also alter the colour that results.

Each system will have its own specific instructions but there are some general principles to follow. The first and most important is preparation: you need to clean the area around the damage as thoroughly as you can, and some kits will provide solvents to help in this regard. Secondly, while most products request users to shake the bottle well before use, with paint they *really* mean it – if it asks you to shake vigorously for three minutes, do exactly that – you can't over-shake paint by hand. Finally, the biggest mistake people make is adding too much paint in one step, which can lead to longer dry times, poor adhesion and unsatisfactory visual results. Always apply multiple thin layers of paint and build the finish up gradually.

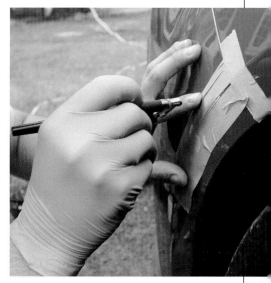

⬆ Professionals use spray application of paint for a higher quality of finish.

⬇ Paint fade is still common in some cars, remove a decal or sticker and you may be amazed - but paint tech has improved massively since the 1990s.

APPENDICES

COMPETITIVE DETAILING

We clean and detail our cars for a multitude of reasons – be it to preserve their value, keep up with the neighbours, distract us from the stresses and vices of life, or simply because we enjoy the physical process and take satisfaction from the results. However, some like to take it a step further and turn it into a competition, and these competitions have become steadily more popular and hard-fought over the years.

At one end of the spectrum you have the 'arrive and shine' where you turn up at a car show and enter your steed into a contest on the day. Car clubs sometimes organise slightly more serious competitions, often referred to as 'show and shines', where competitors need to pre-book their slot and are often split into different categories based on vehicle type or owner experience. At the very top of the tree you have concours competitions, where owners have to battle to get their car entered in the first place, with many events being invitation only. These are normally held at annual meets of the larger car and driver clubs, or very exclusive gatherings such as Salon Privé, Villa d'Este and perhaps the most revered of all, Pebble Beach.

⬇ Salon Privé is one of the UK's most revered concours events.

➡ Good concours judges will examine the car in minute detail, many are professional detailers.

The arrive and shine style shows are normally focussed on cleanliness, so the key to victory is ensuring every single nut and bolt is spotless. As they get more serious, judges look at paint presentation and attention to detail – if you have wax residue in a window seal you will be marked down, the same goes for a dirty undercarriage, hence the use of mirrors on show stands.

The concours is a different beast entirely, and while detailing plays a major part, judges are normally sticklers for originality. This means a car with original paint and patina will always score above flawless, non-original paint. Equally, items like the original owner's handbook and tool kit can make or break a contender, which are often out of the hands of a detailer. That said, a concours detailer will be expected to assist in more pedantic processes than a typical commercial detailer, such as ensuring the head studs on an engine line up correctly and trace of dirt from the tread of a tyre is removed.

⬆ Waxstock is Europe's largest event dedicated to detailing.

We have seen people remove engines to clean them in preparation for concours, but then, a win can add serious value to a classic vehicle, so detailing budgets tend to be in four or five figures.

Ultimately, if you want to show off your handiwork, there are plenty of avenues to go down. The first step would be to join some owners' clubs, either specific to the make (and possibly model) of car you have, or drivers' clubs, which are normally segmented by the period of vehicle (vintage, classic, retro, etc.). The UK plays host to a show called Waxstock, which is dedicated to detailing, rather than having detailing-related side-shows. It is usually held at the Ricoh Arena in summer and is well worth a visit for topping up your supplies, getting involved in the community and learning about the latest products and techniques.

TRAINING

While researching detailing and reading up on car care will help, as well as putting the principles into practice on your own, it can be really beneficial to get some proper hands-on training. There are dozens of training courses available and they fall broadly into three categories:

⬇ Training courses are often held by manufacturers.

Manufacturer courses

These are often free or not very expensive and can be useful for teaching both the basics and more advanced, product-specific techniques. Conversely, they are primarily there to help companies sell product, so they don't always teach the most efficient techniques, and will usually only focus on a single range of products and a single way of doing something.

↑ The UK Detailing Academy offers structured group and one-to-one training.

Independent detailer courses

Quite a few professional detailers offer training courses on the side to supplement their day jobs. These are normally held in small groups or on a one-to-one basis and may not suffer from the product bias of a commercial course. However, rarely are they taught to a structured syllabus, and you need to be sure that the detailer teaching you actually knows what he or she is doing – online stardom is not always an accurate measure of knowledge. Also, check that they hold the relevant professional indemnity and work insurances, as many demonstrate on customer vehicles, and you may be unprotected should things go wrong.

Car care training centres

The UK plays host to a small number of dedicated training centres for detailing such as the UK Detailing Academy, where a range of courses are offered to both the amateur and professional to hone their skills. These benefit from peer-reviewed curriculums, structured learning programmes, trainers who are qualified to teach, manufacturer independence and hold correct insurance. However, there aren't many of them and being professional training centres, don't expect them to be "cheap" - though you can sometimes get government funding if unemployed or leaving the Armed Forces.

GOING PRO

Almost all car care professionals start out as amateurs, and for many it is the appeal of doing what they love and being their own boss that makes the career move very attractive. However, many also underestimate the difference between occasionally cleaning their own car on a sunny Saturday afternoon, and working all hours on customer cars. A fair comparison would be home baking compared to running a commercial kitchen – when you rely on it to pay your bills, it runs the risk of being less enjoyable.

⬇ The PVD Trade Association supports and assesses car care professionals in the UK.

The first step to starting a car care business is to get some formal training from a reputable training centre, many of whom will be able to provide you with both a technical grounding in commercial car care and a guide as to how to go about starting your business. The Professional Valeters and Detailers Trade Association (PVD) is a not-for-profit trade membership that can also assist you in creating a business plan and ensuring you are covering every base. There are pre-requisites with additional theory and practical assessments required for entry that will put you on the map as a Car Care Professional.

FURTHER READING

The most comprehensive work on detailing in recent years is *Automotive Detailing: In Detail* by Dom Colbeck, Jon Steele and David McLean (The Crowood Press Ltd, 2017). There are various publications by American detailer Mike Philips that are particularly useful for those learning about machine polishing. For a quick reference, the *Detailers Dictionary* by Christopher Evans (Bookbaby, 2019) is often handy. Finally, *PRO Detailer Magazine* provides a glut of information for both amateurs and professionals on a regular basis through guides, articles and intensive product testing.

➡ The DetailingWiki site is run from the Netherlands and is a great free source of information.

⬇ The PRO Detailer Magazine is suitable for both professionals and enthusiasts, with back issues forming an encyclopedia of information.

The internet is awash with websites offering all sorts of advice and guidance, with YouTube being a major source of information, but also forums such as Detailing World. As with anything on the internet, take great care to pick reliable sources and always validate the information you are finding from multiple sources. DetailingWiki is managed from the Netherlands and provides a strong source of information.

ACRONYMS

Generic chemical terms

AIO   All In One (type of polish)
APC   All-Purpose Cleaner (detergent product)
DAT   Diminishing Abrasive Technology (polishing compound)
IPA   Isopropyl Alcohol (used in glass cleaners, panel wipe, et al.)
LSP   Last Stage Product (normally a wax, sealant, or coating)
QD   Quick Detailer (spray-on cleaning/gloss-enhancing product)
SMAT   Super Micro Abrasive Technology (polishing compound)
TFR   Traffic Film Remover (genre of cleaning product)
VOC   Volatile Organic Compound (a harmful type of solvent)

Generic hardware terms

CCT   Correlated Colour Temperature (rating for light sources)
CRI   Colour Rendering Index (rating for light sources)
DA   Dual Action (polishing machine)
DI   Deionisation (type of resin used in water filters)
MF   Microfibre (material cloths and some pads are made of)
PTG   Paint Thickness Gauge (sometimes called PDG – paint depth gauge)
RO   Reverse Osmosis (water filtration system)

DILUTIONS

Dilutions are something you will encounter regularly when using detailing chemicals. They will either be displayed as a ratio (x:X or as PIR (Panel Impact Ratio). Both are easy to work out.

For ratios; add both numbers together (e.g. a 1:9 dilution would give you 10) and divide that by your container size. So a 1l bottle would be 1000ml, divided by 10 = 100ml. 1 part (100ml) of chemical to the remainder (900ml) of water gives you your correctly diluted chemical. The first number is always the additive, the second the diluant.

PIR is slightly more involved as you need to work out the Total Volume Output (TVO) of your pressure washer.

To do this. Use your pressure washer and lance to fill an empty bucket with water for 1 minute, then measure how much water is in the bucket. This is your TVO in litres per minute.

Now we divide this number by 100, to give us a 1% PIR figure. Multiply this by the PIR figure on the instructions to give you measure of product you need to use in your lance. For instance;

A PIR of 5% through a lance and pressure washer setup, measured at 4800ml TVO would be: 4800/100 x 5 = 240ml VIL of product Top up with 760ml of water to fill your 1 litre snow foam lance bottle.

ACKNOWLEDGEMENTS

Photo Acknowledgements
Bert Youell - Pro Detailer Magazine
Ian Sealey - Pro Detailer Magazine
Mathew Bedworth - MDB Images

Thanks To
Alan Medcraf - AMDetails
Andrew Southall - Detailed By Andrew
Beth Smith
Bob Turner - HeadTurners Detailing
Charlie Long
Craig Brigham - The Detailing Detectives
Daniel Kiff - Kiffs Valeting & Detailing
Dave Whitehouse - Ideal Valeting
David Guy - Perfectly Polished
Gareth Fisher - Xceed Valeting & Detailing
James Keely - UK Detailing Academy
Jason Burt - Privilege Detail
Jon Delieu - The Forensic Detailing Channel
Jon Imrie - i-4detail
Jonathan Beattie
Justyna Brys - JB Car Detail
Mark Jones
Mark Lister - DDB Detailing
Matt Coyle - Dark Hound Autocare
Nick Fisher - Max Car Care
Nicola Reed - FiftyFive Details
Owain Quick - Mad About Detailing
Peter Davies - Design by Detail
Petri Tiirikainen - Apex Nürburg
Ram Iyer
Richard March - UK Detailing Academy
Rob Rich - Bristol Auto Detailing
Shay Shannon - My Beautiful Car
Steve Bower - Waxworks Professional Valeting & Detailing
Stuart Staples - Auto-Genie
Tim Bomford - Envy Car Care
Tom Morrison-Jones - Ecurie Esprit

INDEX